*Especially for y[...]
that make life spe[...]
for letting me share [...]
you. Much love
Hugs
Carolyn Jackson*

WE
INTERRUPT
THIS
PROGRAM...

CAROLYN JACKSON

WITH

BARBARA BARRIER

EAKIN PRESS ⚡ Austin, Texas

For CIP
information,
please access:
www.loc.gov

FIRST EDITION
Copyright © 2002
By Carolyn Jackson
Published in the United States of America
By Eakin Press
A Division of Sunbelt Media, Inc.
P.O. Drawer 90159 ☍ Austin, Texas 78709-0159
email: sales@eakinpress.com
💻 website: www.eakinpress.com 💻
ALL RIGHTS RESERVED.

1 2 3 4 5 6 7 8 9

1-57168-653-3

Dedicated to:

God, Who makes all things possible;
My precious family—the joy of my life;
Jean, who planted the seed;
Friends, who have stood with me through triumph and tragedy;
Those in this book who touched my life and helped me to grow; and
to Barbara, whose endless hours of work, constant encouragement
and prayers made this labor of love a reality.
—CAROLYN JACKSON

My heartfelt thanks to Carolyn, who lived her incredible life;
to Jesse, who displayed endless love and patience with our project;
and to Marilyn, who promised to buy a book, if I'd just write one.
—BARBARA BARRIER

CONTENTS

PREFACE

This is a book about joy and responsibility and faith. The joy came from my relationship, with my co-workers, listeners, and viewers. It came from knowledge that I was sharing useful information about myriad subjects.

It came from interviewing interesting guests, thus allowing my listeners and viewers a peek into their lives. It came from knowing I entertained and frequently brought sunshine into sometimes lonely lives.

But all the joy was balanced by responsibility. The years have not shaken my belief that persons in my profession always must be fair in our reporting. We never should force our opinions on others, but allow them the freedom to listen and then to make their own judgments.

We should remember our influence often is more far-reaching than we ever imagine and like it or not, we are role models to many people, young and old. We represent our station twenty-four hours a day, whether on duty or not, and we are responsible for our speech and behavior whenever we are in the public eye.

Finally, I know I could not have experienced this joy and responsibility had I not been sustained by a strong faith in God. Television is not always the glamorous world that it appears. There were many times when my world was rocked by insecurity, frustration, disillusionment, and disappointment.

I often felt abandoned in a vast desert. But when I looked closely at the sand through which it seemed I alone was struggling,

I could see but one set of footprints, and I knew the Lord was carrying me through the storms to a bright victory.

Secure in my faith, I was free to give myself up to the joy and
personal satisfaction that appearing on radio and television brought
to my life.

At the request of many friends, I want to share some of the
most meaningful experiences of my career with you.

—CAROLYN JACKSON

"Fame is vapor; popularity an accident, riches take wings. Only one thing endures, and that is character."
—HORACE GREELEY

Laughing it up with Bob Hope.

CHAPTER 1

TAKING OFF

Life will be an adventure for me—starting today.
—SCHOOL POSTER

Bob Hope might be a king in the entertainment world, but he was no match for the space shuttle that day in May 1974. Interviewing him may have been the most important thing in the world to me, but not to Walter Cronkite and CBS.

There I stood, at the pinnacle of my broadcasting career. I was on one side of the microphone, Bob Hope on the other. It was my dream interview come true. In between swings during Austin's Legends of Golf tournament, the legendary Bob was just about to answer all my carefully framed questions.

Suddenly, across the screen flashed the words that usually herald some earth-shaking event: "We interrupt this program . . ." and Walter rattled off a routine update on the shuttle crew's antics. You know, they had Tang for breakfast and did their morning exercises. After analyzing the crew's activities for about six minutes, Mr. Cronkite returned programming to the local station.

Alas, all the audience heard from Bob and me were my closing remarks. The precious interview was lost forever. Don't misunderstand, I was as interested in the space program as any other good American citizen. And, I welcomed television coverage of the

Bob Hope gives Carolyn some golf pointers.

Following Bob Hope around Austin's Onion Creek Golf Course.

events. But to interrupt regular programming merely to tell us about the astronauts' breakfast, exercise routine, etc., was a bit much. And, leave it to the thorough Walter, after reporting the activities, he recapped them and then analyzed them!

In this business, you win a few and you lose a few. At least I fulfilled my long-time dream of meeting Bob Hope, and I treasure the memory in my heart, along with so many other experiences that graced my twenty years in Central Texas communications, radio, and television.

However, it was another interview that led me to write this book. Some years ago, I was talking with psychic Jean Dixon when she interrupted our conversation to say, "My dear, if you're ever going to know fame and fortune, you must get into the right profession."

Shocked, I replied, "I thought I *was* in the right profession. If it's not television, then what is it?"

"You should be writing."

"Writing? I can't write."

"That's your stumbling block—you think you can't. Yes, yes, you *can* write. There's a story there, and someday you'll tell it."

So, Jean, here I am, telling my story.

* * *

My dad said I was born talking. I didn't ask just the usual "Why, Daddy?" questions. I had to know the who, what, when, and where about everything and everybody. It was a trait that served me well as I groped toward the career that awaited me.

I was not a shy child—my older brother, Marvin, was. He was so withdrawn my mother thought it would help him to take expression. I was only four or five years old, and baby sitters were unheard of in those days, so I accompanied him and Mother and absorbed every one of his lessons.

On recital night, Marvin decided he just could not perform in front of all those people. He knew his piece very well, but he wasn't about to get up on that stage and say it in public. Guess who volunteered to perform in his place? Right. And the teacher let me.

I loved performing, especially the applause and the attention it brought. The die was cast. I may not have realized it at that tender age, but my life's direction was set.

Brother Marvin and Carolyn — which one loves the spotlight?

* * *

Certain people have a powerful impact on our lives, even though we may not understand it at the time. During my formative years, two gentlemen played key roles in motivating me and helping to establish my self-esteem.

When I was about ten years old, our family experienced an extremely difficult time. The Great Depression was taking its toll on my parents, and their financial struggles strained their marriage nearly to the breaking point. I couldn't imagine my future being bright or offering me any unique opportunities. I felt frightened and confused, but I had no one to talk to about my fears. My brother and I bottled up our concerns within ourselves and didn't even discuss them with each other.

Papa Young, our school custodian, sensed that I was deeply troubled. All the kids adored him because of his sweet smile and pleasant manner. He was stern and authoritative, but kind and understanding. One day he singled me out for the honor of ringing the school bell at recess. As we sat talking, he asked, "Carolyn, what's your favorite subject?"

"Geography," I replied, breathlessly. "I want to see Hawaii and the volcanoes and Holland and the windmills and tulips and the glaciers in Alaska and all the other wonderful places we study." Deep inside, I believed travel was never to be a part of my life. How could a little girl from Taylor, Texas, whose family's modest income provided few opportunities, ever manage to wander the world?

Papa Young took my hand and said, "Look out there over those trees and into that blue sky. That's the world, Carolyn, and it's yours. Your whole life is ahead of you, and it's going to be wonderful.

"You're a very smart, friendly young lady and you have loads of personality. If you believe you can, and you work hard enough, you can go anywhere and do anything you want to do. The world is yours for the taking."

That dear man changed my life that day. I believed him, and all I needed was a nudge from an adult I admired and respected, one who was wise, kind, and knew about the world, and who believed in me. Suddenly, I could visualize myself taking advantage of the marvels of the world. After all, Papa Young said I could do it, and he wouldn't lie to me.

Then there was the matter of freckles. My best friend was a miniature Elizabeth Taylor, beautiful from head to toe—plus, she was talented. She could tap dance like Shirley Temple and was an extremely graceful ballet and toe dancer.

I didn't resent her—quite the contrary. I adored her. But as a skinny strawberry blonde with freckles, I soon got the message that perhaps I was an ugly duckling. You might say I was totally lacking in the self-esteem department, thinking that self-worth and ability were based on beauty alone.

But an artist changed all that. He was the cousin of a friend, and one day he offered to draw a sketch of me to give to my parents.

That sounded like fun, so I perched myself on a stool, dazzled him with my best smile, and asked him please not to put my freckles in the picture.

"Why not?" he asked, looking puzzled.

"Because they're ugly."

"Don't you realize what freckles are?"

"Yes, they're ugly brown spots."

"No, my dear. Those are personality dots, and the more you

Elizabeth Taylor look-alike friend Lou Ann Harkins and Carolyn, all grown up.

have, the more personality you have. God has truly blessed you with all that personality.

"People will be drawn to you like a magnet. Even though the freckles may fade in time, you'll have that fantastic personality forever."

In an instant, that man revolutionized my perception of myself. Never again did I view my freckles with loathing. I just thanked the Lord for all the abundant evidence of personality He had given me. I realized that perhaps my worth would not be measured by my beauty or lack thereof.

To this day, I thank my friend's cousin for teaching me what self-esteem was all about. Years later, the memories of those people who believed in me came into sharp focus when I found myself in the limelight of Central Texas radio and television.

Role models meant so much to me, I never wanted to say or do anything that would be in bad taste or project the wrong image. To enjoy the privileges that came with being a radio and television personality, I also had to accept the responsibilities that accompanied the package. That meant I would have to become a good role model myself. Little did I know to what lengths that decision sometimes would take me.

One day, shortly after I began my television career in Austin, a little boy's mother called me. The next week was Public Education Week, and parents and friends were invited to visit the schools. The mother explained her son had seen me on television and was obsessed with the idea that I be his guest at school.

"I know how busy you are, but could you possibly find time to visit his school next Thursday afternoon?" she pleaded. "It's right off Braker Lane."

"I don't get off the air until 12:30 P.M., and the station may place some demands on my time that day, but I will try. No promises, though," I replied.

Thursday was a nightmare. My guest failed to show and everything was chaotic. Totally drained, I just wanted to go home, kick off my shoes, and relax. However, on my way home, when I reached Braker Lane, I found myself turning off the highway.

In front of the school, a little boy waited alone on the curb. He was clutching a flower. Shyly handing it to me, he breathlessly introduced himself, then took me inside and proudly presented me to his teacher and his class. He was the most charming and attentive date I'd ever had.

To his utter delight, I visited with the children and explained a little bit about my world of radio and television.

Driving home after my visit with that enchanting child and his friends, I cried. What if I had left that precious little boy sitting on that curb? Instead, I believe God nudged me into accepting his invitation, and I shared a magical moment with that little boy. I hope it was as special to him as it was to me.

Even through the days when ratings seemed to hinge on how controversial a broadcast personality could be, I clung to my decision never to betray my viewers' trust in me.

CHAPTER 2
FLASHBACK

Nothing is waste that makes a memory.
—"Star Tips," D. Modin

In junior high and high school, I'd never heard of ratings and had no inkling how vitally they would affect my career. I just knew I wanted to perform.

Speech, drama, choir—anything that had to do with performing—drew me like a moth to light. I loved competing in meets. I also assumed leadership roles in activities such as student council.

I enjoyed the social aspects of teenage life, too. I was never voted "Most Beautiful," but I did nab "Most Popular." It must have been those personality dots.

Graduation was both happy and sad. It was difficult leaving behind my memorable high school years, but the University of Texas beckoned, and I was excited and ready to plunge into the next phase of life.

Like most university freshmen, I didn't have a definite degree plan, but I knew I wanted to pursue a career in speech. I should have guessed how rocky my career road was going to be when I discovered the only speech degree plan at UT was aimed at teachers and therapists. Fortunately, this lack was remedied during my sophomore year when the school added a broadcasting degree plan to its curriculum.

Carolyn — Cheerleader for the Fighting Taylor Ducks.

There were no so-called "professors of broadcasting" in those days, so we were taught by people from the broadcasting industry—what a plus! There wasn't much textbook work either—another plus. The best part was we were allowed to tap into the experiences of these people who knew the ropes.

The principles of broadcasting were different then. We were taught that advertising was always to be positive, never negative. Too bad that rule fell by the wayside.

Tom Rishworth, director of the broadcasting school, emphasized the importance of developing a pleasing voice and perfect pronunciation. Grammatical errors were not tolerated.

Dr. DeWitt Reddick, head of the journalism department, stressed ethics and professionalism repeatedly, drumming into us that we must learn the difference between editorializing and news reporting. This is a tenet many of today's television anchor people apparently failed to absorb in school. Or maybe they don't teach that anymore.

At last, I completed the degree I sought. Proudly clutching my diploma, I hunted a job.

Station KTAE in Taylor, Texas, gave me my first job after graduating from UT in January 1948, but I only stayed there five months because the next summer I took off for Evanston, Illinois, where I had been accepted to Northwestern University's National Broadcasting Company Institute.

This unique opportunity offered me a chance to earn graduate credit while taking courses taught by NBC personnel. The institute accepted just 100 students per summer for the training, and I felt very fortunate to have been chosen.

I believe I was offered the chance to attend the institute because Tom Rishworth recommended me. Tom had worked for NBC for thirty years before taking the broadcast department director's position at UT. He still had great clout at NBC, and I was flattered he had such faith in my ability.

When I finished the course, I, along with my roommates, Julie Dossett from Tennessee and Shirley Myers from Missouri, decided to stay in Chicago to seek our fortunes, much to my mother's dismay. I was way ahead of the times, because in those days most girls didn't do that. Those who had to work taught school, became nurses, or did secretarial work. Otherwise, they settled down, got married, and reared a family.

Carolyn and roommate Mary Louise Smith hit the books at UT.

Chicago roommates Carolyn; Shirley Myers, Missouri; B. J. Holcombe, Nebraska; and Julie Dossett, Tennessee; sing favorite state songs.

My mother was beside herself when I broke the news I'd be staying in the Windy City.

"Call her and tell her she has to come home," Mother insisted to Dad.

"No! She's twenty-one, has a degree from UT, and she's not asking us for money, so we can't tell her what to do. She can do whatever she damn well pleases," Dad firmly replied. He was way ahead of his time, too.

I went to work in Chicago for the Leo Burnett Advertising Agency's research department. I didn't really want to do research—that sounded dull. However, it got my foot in the door, and I believed that in time I could move into radio/television production.

After a few months, I was intrigued with advertising research. Every day was a new challenge, and I never knew what I'd be doing next.

One of my first assignments was researching the old Bobbi home permanent. It was a good product, but it wasn't selling, even though we had launched an aggressive advertising campaign. Visiting various department stores, I found out why. When I'd ask for a Bobbi perm, the saleswoman was likely to say, "Oh, you won't like that permanent. Why don't you try a Toni instead?" I discovered immediately that lack of education for the sales force was at the root of the problem.

Television was in its infancy then, and one of my other duties with Leo Burnett was researching the audience appeal of children's television programs. Amazingly, at that time we had a list of everyone in Chicago who had a television set. Howdy Doody was just about the only children's television show airing, so I'd call parents and ask them their opinions of the program.

Life in Chicago's fast lane was enticing, and I found my research duties more interesting than I had expected, but Chily, my high school sweetheart, had completed his hitch in the navy and was waiting for me. I went home to Taylor, Texas, and we were married in July 1949.

As a happy new bride, I didn't dream my faith was about to be tested in the most devastating manner.

My brother and his wife had a baby girl, Linda. She was the first baby in our family since I was born, so you can imagine all the attention focused on this little blonde, blue-eyed doll. A lot of that attention came from me, because most everyone said she was my little miniature, which pleased me immensely.

I would dream up reasons to baby-sit with her because every moment I spent in her company was so precious to me.

But then Linda developed leukemia, and when she was two and a half years old, she died. I thought God had betrayed me, because bad things weren't supposed to happen to good people.

It didn't seem fair. I thought my family and I *were* good people. We tried to do what was right. We tried not to hurt anyone. We tried to be honest and help people. And yet, this terrible thing had happened to us. I had begged God to heal Linda, and instead she died on my birthday.

Niece Linda Gossett with her mom, Lorraine.

I went through all the emotions. Disbelief, realization, the need to blame. I chose to blame God. I was angry with God—so angry. After all, He allowed this tragedy to happen. I had a very distorted view of death. It was centered on myself, my loss, my grief. I buried my agony deep inside, sharing it with no one.

Chily and I continued to live in Taylor. Time passed, and we were blessed with two beautiful daughters, Cindi and Carol, who later provided us with five wonderful grandchildren.

I stayed home and cared for our two little girls while Chily went into business with my father. They operated a Purina feed and grain dealership in Taylor.

Both of us were doing well, but we decided we needed a change of scene.

Chily went to work directly for Ralston-Purina in their sales department, and we moved to LaGrange, near the center of Chily's territory. A year later, Chily was made manager of a large Ralston-

Purina company-owned store in San Antonio, so we moved there, and the girls started to school.

With Chily consumed with his new job and the girls settled into school, I found myself with time on my hands. Restlessness overcame me, and I longed for a new challenge.

While pondering what I might do to add some excitement to my life, I paced the floor and tried to think of something, anything that I might tackle. Nothing. Nada. My mind was blank. No inspiring revelations.

Finally, I decided to play Scarlet and worry about it tomorrow. I poured another cup of coffee, opened the *San Antonio Express-News,* and lost myself in the daily news.

Immediately, my eyes focused on a big article about the search for a woman to represent the State of Texas at CBS Daytime Televisit Week. I couldn't read fast enough.

The essence of the article was that CBS Television was asking each state to send a representative to New York and Los Angeles to visit the sets of daytime TV shows, interview the stars and producers, then file daily stories for local newspapers. *The San Antonio Express-News* and KENS-TV (CBS affiliate) were the sponsors for Texas. Any interested woman was to submit a letter of twenty-five words or less stating why she should be chosen. My wheels were already turning.

By the time Chily got home that evening, I was totally submerged in my creative endeavor at the typewriter. Of course, he inquired what I was doing.

Nonchalantly, I replied, "Oh, nothing important."

But he knew by the determined look on my face that I was up to something. After a few minutes, he said, "I bet I know what you're doing. You're entering that TV contest. Don't you realize nobody ever wins those things?"

That did it. I was more determined than ever to win that contest.

The most popular TV show at the time was *Have Gun, Will Travel,* so my entry was a takeoff on that. Example: "Have broadcasting degree from University of Texas—will travel. Have experience in industry—will travel," etc.

Mailing in my entry, I waited not so patiently for the reply. It came one morning while I was washing the breakfast dishes. I was one of the five finalists and would meet with a panel of judges the next day for an interview.

My adrenaline was in overdrive. I didn't sleep a wink that night, worrying about the interview and what I would wear. Not that I had a lot of choices. Reaching into the closet the next morning, I grabbed my only suit, hoped the butterflies would go away, and headed for my interview.

The panel of judges consisted of the mayor of San Antonio, several TV station executives, and some bigwigs from the newspaper. After all the interviews were finished, we five finalists nervously waited for the results. The wait seemed an eternity, but actually was only about thirty minutes. Finally, the door opened, out came the judges, and the announcment was made.

The winner—*me!*

My knees almost buckled as they snapped a picture of the mayor pinning a corsage on me—a photo-op for the newspaper.

I trembled all the way home, wept tears of joy, drove a bit too fast, and thanked God for providing me with such a fabulous opportunity.

Chily was waiting for me when I got home. I dashed into the house, tears still streaming down my face, and couldn't resist saying, "Remember those contests that nobody ever wins? Well, somebody does—*me!*"

We rarely went out to eat in those days, but this called for a celebration, so the Jackson family went out for a very special dinner.

As the reality of my upcoming adventure soaked in, I realized I was facing two huge challenges—flying (I had never been on an airplane before, and I would be flying to New York, then to Los Angeles, and back home) and writing daily newspaper articles—never before had my journalistic abilities been tested.

Chily's mom arrived to run the household for me. I borrowed some clothes from my sister-in-law to fill the gaps in my wardrobe, and I was ready for my adventure. I was still terrified at the thought of flying, but after about twenty minutes in the air, I was hooked. I knew I was destined to be a frequent flyer.

The trip far exceeded my expectations. I felt like a queen, not for a day, but for a week. One of the greatest unexpected pleasures was meeting and getting to know the ladies from the other forty-nine states. We had lots of late-night gab fests and in no time felt as though we'd been friends forever, a bond many of us would share for years to come.

The excitement and glamour of visiting TV sets (mostly soap operas) and interviewing those involved was like nothing I had ever experienced. Much to my surprise, the thing that thrilled me most was meeting the deadline of writing my daily stories, wiring them to the *Express News*, and knowing that my family and friends were vicariously enjoying the trip with me.

Thoughts of my family were ever-present, and I was quick to seize the opportunity to get autographs for the girls from Captain Kangaroo and Mr. Green Jeans when we visited their delightful set.

After four whirlwind days in New York, we headed for Los Angeles for more royal treatment. All fifty of us were guests on the Art Linkletter show, and he singled out three of us to answer questions about our state.

His question for me was, "What is your state flower?—and spell it." Oops. Of course, I knew it was the bluebonnet, but suddenly I had brain fade. I always used to win the spelling bees, so why suddenly could I not remember whether it had one *N*, two *N's* and how many *T's?*

Realizing I would be excommunicated from the Lone Star State if I missed this question on national TV, I snapped my brain back from the fuzzy zone and spelled bluebonnet—correctly. For that few minutes of agony, I won a fantastic vacuum cleaner and lots of applause.

Perhaps the highlight of the LA trip was the farewell dinner where we were greeted by Ronald and Nancy Reagan and then hobnobbed with some of the TV stars. How good could it get?

For weeks after the trip, I pinched myself to make sure I was awake and all this had not been just a fantastic dream. But the personal notes to Cindi and Carol from Captain Kangaroo and Mr. Green Jeans proudly displayed on the refrigerator were constant reminders that yes, the trip was real.

I learned a valuable lesson during that venture. Go for it, no matter what the odds; you just might win.

Once I returned from cloud nine and resumed a normal life, my thoughts turned to, "What now?" Chily and the girls were my first priority, but I knew I could balance family and some outside interest.

After considering several options, I decided I would like to substitute teach. That would only require my being away from home

Art Linkletter shares a light moment with participants in the CBS Daytime Televisit Week.

the same hours as the girls and would allow me the freedom to participate in all their activities.

I signed up and was called immediately. I became such a regular at the girls' school, the principal urged me to teach full time, but I couldn't, because I lacked the proper certification. Discovering that I needed just fifteen hours to secure my teaching certificate, I attended Trinity University nights and summers to earn the required hours. When I finished, the principal hired me to teach fifth grade.

Noticing that I was an effective classroom teacher, and being aware of my broadcasting background, my fellow teachers recommended me to KLRN, the Austin public broadcasting television station, as a TV teacher. They did this entirely without my knowledge, but I was excited about the opportunity to audition, because I saw the job as a beautiful blend of two careers.

Unfortunately, the job opening was for a science teacher, and I knew virtually nothing about teaching science. It must have showed, because I didn't get the job.

Meanwhile, Ralston-Purina decided to close its company-owned stores, which meant Chily would have to return to sales, take a salary cut, and develop another territory if he stayed with them.

He left Purina and went into partnership with a man on a commercial egg farm. It did well, but chickens lay eggs every day, and Chily was rarely home.

In the summer of 1965, on our first family vacation in years, Chily and I were watching the sunset at the Grand Canyon when he turned to me and said, "Tutta [my nickname], I'm working such long hours that I'm missing the girls' childhood. And I'm tired of living in a big city. Let's move back to Taylor."

I stared at him. "Fine, but what will we do?"

"Well, you can always teach, and I'll find something." We decided that if we were going to make such a drastic change, we needed to do it then, because older daughter Cindi was about to enter high school, and we didn't want to move her once she began. Chily sold his business, and we packed up and returned to Taylor.

Chily did his homework and learned that Taylor needed a dry-cleaning establishment and a washateria, so he opened one. I applied for a teaching job and was assigned a fourth-grade class.

I had an ethnically mixed classroom in a school that offered fewer advantages than the affluent school where I had taught in San Antonio, so the change was an adjustment. But I welcomed the challenge and enjoyed my work.

I taught in Taylor for a year. Then, out of the blue, I had a call from KLRN, the public television station. They were planning to offer a libraries and literature television course to third- through sixth-grade classrooms, and they invited me to audition to teach it.

This time I landed the job, and it was perfect for me. Gordon Smith, my director, and I were afforded a great deal of creative freedom as long as we stayed within the guidelines of the curriculum.

We designed a little model library, and through the magic of television's special effects, I was able to grow small and take the children inside with me and teach them how to use it.

We studied the Dewey decimal system, using puppets. I introduced the students to good literature by inviting drama students to act out scenes or to read aloud. Sometimes I interviewed the authors of award-winning children's books.

After teaching on public television for three years, my big break finally came. I heard that Jean Boone, hostess for a women's program on KTBC—then Austin's only local TV station—was leaving her position.

Deciding it was time to return to commercial broadcasting, I auditioned for Jean's job. To do this, I had to work live on the air with the station's program director, the legendary Cactus Pryor, as my co-host. The station narrowed the field to five candidates, and then each of us had to work live on the air alone for a week. The viewers then were invited to send in their opinions. To my delight, viewer reaction was overwhelmingly in my favor.

"I'd like to have her for a friend—she seems like the girl next door," was representative of viewers' comments.

As Cactus was fond of saying, "We didn't choose Carolyn because she was the most beautiful. We chose her because she was the one the viewers liked."

Truthfully, I was safe to watch. Women liked me because I wasn't a sex symbol. I wasn't beautiful enough to be a threat. Men enjoyed the program because it was informative, intelligent, and fun, and their wives wouldn't get mad if they watched.

So I snagged the job as hostess of *Woman's World*, and I was scheduled to start in a week. The reality didn't hit for a few days, and then I ran the gamut of emotions—fright, excitement, anticipation, panic.

In spite of my excitement, leaving KLRN was hard because I had loved my work there. A comment from one of my co-workers boosted my spirits and heightened my anticipation.

"This has renewed my faith in this profession. I know you didn't sleep with anyone to get the job," he told me. "You got it because you're good."

CHAPTER 3
SO THIS IS TV?

You'll never face a problem that's not charged with opportunity.
—"P.S. I LOVE YOU"

Not only was I going to be on live TV five days a week, but I would be employed by a station owned by Lady Bird Johnson, wife of President Lyndon Baines Johnson. A unique position!

The Johnsons owned the station and the building. They maintained a penthouse on the fifth floor that was their home when in Austin for business or social functions. Their main home was the LBJ Ranch, about forty-five miles west of Austin.

When the Johnsons were in the penthouse at the station, Secret Service men were always close by. Usually a couple of them sat in the reception area.

They were there the day I went for my meeting with J. C. Kellam, general manager of KTBC. Little did I know when they introduced themselves that they would become dear friends, for whom I would have the utmost respect.

Mr. Kellam, lifelong close friend of President Johnson, set up an appointment with me before I assumed my duties, to welcome me and to discuss the show.

"Mrs. Jackson," (he always called me Mrs. Jackson, never Carolyn) "this is your program. You are in full control. I know you will exhibit good taste in your choice of subject matter and guests. All I ask of you is that within the next year your name become a household word in Central Texas."

The first task was to meet everyone on staff, learn where their offices were, and move into my working spot. I loved my office. It was on the fourth floor, a rather secluded spot away from the main hustle and bustle of the station. Though it wasn't large, just room for a desk, bookshelf, a couple of chairs, and a full-length mirror, it was bright and cheerful.

I immediately added touches to lend it my signature. I installed a bulletin board to post all my favorite sayings. Pictures of my guests and me decked the walls. Favorite family photos and special mementos graced my desk.

And—the finishing touch—a six-foot cutout of Burt Reynolds in the corner. What fun it was to see the expressions of those who entered my office for the first time! A typical remark: "This isn't an office, it's an adventure."

Finally, the big day came—my debut as hostess of *Woman's World*, in November 1968. To say I had butterflies is the understatement of the year. About ten minutes before airtime, doubt overcame me.

"What am I doing here? What if I make a fool of myself in front of everyone in Central Texas?"

The crew was wonderful. They did everything they could to make me feel comfortable and to ease the tension. As the floor manager gave me the countdown, he also flashed me the biggest, most welcoming smile I'd ever seen.

When the red light flashed on Camera 1, indicating we were on the air, my adrenaline kicked in, fear departed, and I sailed smoothly through my first telecast. By the end of the week, I had settled comfortably into the routine.

I arrived at the studio each day about 9:00 A.M. and spent the morning returning phone calls, scheduling future programs, pre-recording commercials, and preparing for the day's show.

After a brief meeting with my director, I would greet my guest in the coffee shop between 11:00 and 11:30 A.M. We would get acquainted, and I would brief him or her on the format of the show and what to expect in the studio. Guests were usually nervous, so I spent most of the time assuring them the interview

Collecting my thoughts between TV show guests.

would be an enjoyable experience and trying to make them feel comfortable with me. Since cameras have a way of intimidating people, I always advised they ignore the cameras and simply look at me.

Inevitably, after the show, the guest would say, "That wasn't so bad. In fact, it was fun." Afternoons found me answering mail, returning more phone calls, and doing research for the next day's program.

I have to chuckle at today's TV world. At the end of talk shows, they run a long list of credits—producer, associate producer, make-up, etc.

Had they run those credits at the end of my show, the screen would have looked something like this:

- Producer—Carolyn Jackson
- Associate Producer—Carolyn Jackson
- Researcher—Carolyn Jackson
- Makeup—Carolyn Jackson
- Secretary—Carolyn Jackson

Station manager J. C. Kellam (right) joins Carolyn in surprising advertiser and El Rancho restaurant owner Matt Martinez.

Get the picture? I was the whole shooting match as far as planning and preparing the show.

But once I entered the studio, I became a small part of a great team—a fabulous director; courteous, competent cameramen; audio men; lighting men; etc. But you'll notice they were all men. At that time, women were not privy to those jobs. We didn't even have any women in the newsroom. You could say I was in a male-dominated profession. However, they didn't appear to resent me. In fact, most of them became my friends.

After a few months, the studio was as much a home to me as my own living room. Viewers began writing and calling to express their approval of my show. Thankfully, both sexes and all ages seemed to like me, perhaps because they perceived me as a friend.

The ratings soared, which pleased the sales department and management. They were amazed that the ratings revealed I had a large minority following. It didn't surprise me. I didn't choose guests by the color of their skin. I tried to vary the show enough to appeal to all ethnic groups, all ages, and all interests.

It was a gratifying moment when I arrived at my office one day and found a memo from Mr. Kellam:

You are doing an excellent job. We are so fortunate to have you.

You have indeed made Carolyn Jackson a household word! Keep up the good work.

I wasn't making much money, but a pat on the back goes a long way. Besides, I loved what I was doing.

The one thing I was totally unprepared for, though, was the public recognition and the relentless demands on my free time.

Everywhere I went—the grocery store, restaurants, the mall—people stopped and talked to me and asked me for my autograph. It was overwhelming, but I never considered it an intrusion. Instead, I was flattered. But it was then I realized my anonymity was gone, and I had a tremendous responsibility on my shoulders. I added a new saying from a church's order of worship to my bulletin board:

Be careful what you say and do.

You may be the only Bible some people ever read.

Requests for personal appearances began to mount. Every small town in Central Texas had some need for my presence—emcee a pageant, judge a cook-off, ride in a parade. There were endless requests from service clubs, youth groups, or organizations asking me to speak. Most of my weekends were filled trying to accommodate everyone. It paid off. The ratings continued to rise.

Bless my family—I couldn't have done it without their support and understanding. In fact, Chily and/or the girls tried to accompany me to the weekend events whenever possible.

I also was trying to take an active part in all my daughters' school activities, plus trying to spend time with my aging parents. Tritely stated, I was burning the candle at both ends.

It finally caught up with me. One day I fainted on the air—surely a first!

Right in the middle of an interview, I grew dizzy, my guest became a blur, and everything began fading away. I knew something was desperately wrong, and I had to let Dana Martin, the show's director, know. I lowered my head and put my hand to my forehead, hoping Dana would realize it was a signal. He picked up on it immediately and switched to a commercial.

I dimly heard one of the cameramen say, "Are you okay?" With that, I crumpled to the floor. They rushed station personality Jay

Hodgson in to finish the show. Jay tried to be calm and reassuring when he announced that I had become ill and he would continue the show in my place.

The next thing I remember was being carried into the lounge by one of the station's salesmen. He placed me on the sofa, and I came to but was still lightheaded and disoriented. Over my protests, they called an ambulance, and I was rushed to the hospital.

Unfortunately, both Chily and my parents were watching the show and were terrified. Chily made it the thirty-five miles from Taylor to the hospital almost as fast as the ambulance made it from the station.

After undergoing a battery of tests and consulting several doctors, they determined that nothing serious was wrong. They couldn't precisely pinpoint what caused my attack, but possible causes were fatigue, stress, or vertigo. (I had experienced inner ear problems before.)

By the next day, I was back on the air apologizing to the viewers for my sudden disappearance. However, I knew I couldn't keep up my killing pace.

Chily was scheduled to go to Houston for a few days on a business trip. I hadn't planned to go, but changed my mind. Mr. Kellam agreed I needed a couple of days off, so I joined Chily for a long weekend.

We checked into the Houston hotel, and I slept for three days, getting up only to have dinner with Chily each evening. "It was like a weekend with a zombie," he teased.

It was a refreshing retreat. I came back rested, but fully aware I had to slow down. It was hard to accept that I was not Superwoman. Although I still tried to accommodate as many requests as possible, I did learn tactfully to decline when the pressures began to mount.

As the months rolled by, I dedicated my energy to making the show as diverse, informative, and entertaining as possible. Some of the guests were regulars. We had a cooking segment once a week featuring a home economist from Southern Union Gas. This was the crew's favorite segment because whatever she cooked, they ate. Two home economists alternated for a while; then one, Janelle Jones, permanently took over the spot.

Janelle was the Martha Stewart of that era. She and I bonded immediately and our friendship survived all the upheavals of the industry. She even went with me when I moved to another station—more on that later.

Monthly features included an interior designer discussing home decorating; the Austin head librarian reviewing best-sellers; exercise and fitness; and fashion. I added new ones—one was a segment called "Meet the Mayor." I would invite the mayor of one of the surrounding towns to tout his town and acquaint viewers with all it had to offer.

Having local VIPs host the show for me while I was on vacation was a true audience-pleaser. Among the more popular were Carole Keeton Rylander, who was Austin's mayor at the time and who now serves as comptroller for the State of Texas, and the late John Bustin, movie critic for the *Austin American-Statesman*.

One of my pet projects was to have someone from the Department of Human Services show pictures of children available for adoption and to explain each child's needs. It was unbelievable the number of children we were able to place in homes as a result of those programs.

I started an annual tradition of a big Christmas program where

Austin American-Statesman *film critic John Bustin (center) entertains Carolyn and Chily at a Country Dinner Playhouse cocktail party.*

Celebrity tennis tournament pits former Austin mayors Carole Keeton Rylander and Jeff Friedman against KTBC news director Joe Roddy and Carolyn.

I introduced all the staff at the station—the people behind the scenes whom the viewers never saw otherwise. All the staff who could brought their families. Chily and our daughters were always on hand for the festivities. Later, our sons-in-law joined the group, and when our first grandchild was on the way, I announced it on the Christmas show. At the end of those special shows, we all gathered around and sang Christmas carols. The viewers loved it.

I especially enjoyed spotlighting new talent trying to make it to stardom.

Many of them did—I hope my part helped.

Most of all, the viewers were fascinated with celebrities, and I tried to accommodate their interest whenever I could.

CHAPTER 4

SPOTLIGHT ON THE STARS

Everyone you meet knows something you don't know, but
need to know. Learn from them.
— "P.S. I LOVE YOU"

Celebrities! Viewers never could get enough of them. "What are these famous folks really like?" they wanted to know.

The answer is that most of them are very much like you, me, our friends, and relatives. Some are shy, others are bold. Most are courteous, a few are self-centered and rude. Some are easy to interview, others find the process difficult.

Another inevitable question: "Who was your favorite?" That's a tough one, because I met many delightful actors, actresses, sports figures, and statesmen.

If I must name a favorite, it has to be Gregory Peck. He was the epitome of a gentleman, always immaculate, polite, and soft-spoken.

Any time a major production company promoted one of its movies, they brought media people to one location instead of taking the stars on tour. This was called a movie junket. Media people flew in one night, had dinner, viewed the film, and conducted interviews the next day.

I met Gregory Peck on such a junket.

His current movie was *The Omen*. Mine was the last ten-minute slot in the afternoon. Mr. Peck had been interviewed all day long, answering the same boring, tiresome questions.

We talked about the movie and my allotted time quickly ran out.

"We spent the whole time talking about the movie, and I didn't have time to find out about you," I told him.

"Are you in a hurry?" he asked.

"No."

"Let's do another one. You guys put up a new tape," he instructed the crew.

"We're not supposed to do but one," the crew shot back.

"Hey, if Twentieth Century Fox won't pay for it, I will," he replied.

Delighted, I listened while he talked about his family. I discovered that both of us rode tandem bikes. Our kids had just given Chily and me one for Christmas. We talked about how much fun riding one was, and he told me he and his wife had ridden through the south of France.

He talked about LBJ and Lady Bird, and our time together was absolutely delightful.

When the interview ended, turning suddenly serious, Mr. Peck said, "Don't you feel sorry for me?"

"Should I?"

"Yes."

"Why?"

"Because, while I'm sitting here slaving over this interview, do you know where my wife is?"

"No, where?"

Grinning broadly, he replied, "Over at Neiman Marcus, spending all my money."

Another favorite was Charlton Heston. He was very much a gentleman, impeccably groomed, and so easy to talk to.

Mr. Heston went to the dinner with us the night before the interview, which gave us an opportunity to really get to know him. He made us forget we were with a star of that magnitude. We talked about everyday things and current events.

The greatest thing, though, occurred the week after the interview. I received a thank-you letter from Charlton Heston thanking me for taking time to interview him and sharing him and his thoughts with my viewers. That framed letter hangs in my home. To me, it signifies the reason he's a great star—he does little things that show his courtesy and gratitude, and what a fine person he really is.

Maybe it was the freckles, but something told me Stefanie Powers and I would bond. While in Austin starring in a play at St. Edward's University, she came to the station for an interview just before July 4.

My program had two segments. The first segment featured news and public affairs. During the second segment, I interviewed my special guest. The day Stefanie came, I was publicizing Independence Day events in Central Texas. I discovered she had never taken part in any of those things. She had never been to a county fair, a city-wide picnic, or any such event.

"Would you like to go to an old-fashioned July 4 celebration?" I asked.

"Oh, yes, that would be wonderful."

"I would love to take you to TIF Days over in Taylor. Would you like to spend the day with my family?"

"Oh, could I?"

Imagine! Stefanie Powers was going to be my family's guest for the day. I set it up, alerting the Taylor Chamber of Commerce that she might come. If so, we decided she should ride in the lead car in the parade.

Stefanie's mother joined her during her stay in Austin, and they had a car. Sure enough, she drove up in our driveway at 9:30 A.M. on July 4 with her mom and her dog in tow.

We had coffee and debated what to do with the dog. I called my next-door neighbor, who had the same kind of dog. I can only imagine the look on his face when I invited him to come over and have coffee with Stefanie Powers. He was thrilled to dog-sit.

Although Stefanie was casually dressed, had lots of freckles, and wore her hair in a ponytail, she was beautiful. She led the July 4 parade in Taylor, ate barbecue on a paper plate, and had the time of her life. After lunch we went to the arts and crafts festival. When people recognized her, they were not intrusive, but they were star-struck. She was very gracious and talked to everyone.

Too soon it was over, and she had to return to Austin for her performance.

"This has been one of the most fun days of my life—a day I'll never forget," she told me warmly as she hugged us good-bye.

The city of Taylor and I will never forget it, either. Just recently, a man stopped me and said he'd never forget shaking hands with Stefanie Powers when she spent July 4 in Taylor.

I interviewed Nancy Reagan before Ronald Reagan became president. She was in Austin for only one day. The Republican Women called and asked me to interview her. I jumped at the opportunity, as Mr. Reagan had not yet announced his candidacy for president, but it was evident that he would.

As we got acquainted in the coffee shop prior to the taping, I sensed she was ill at ease.

"Mrs. Reagan, I am not a news reporter. I host a family-oriented show. My goal is to spotlight my guests. I believe that if my guest enjoys himself or herself, my viewers will enjoy it, too.

"If there's anything you don't want to talk about, that will be fine, as it's not my style to embarrass anyone."

She seemed to realize she could trust me and looked me straight in the eye. "Ask me anything you want to," she said.

I tried to focus on topics that would reveal the real Nancy Reagan, and she positively beamed when I asked about her pet project, her "Adopt a Grandparent" program.

After our interview, whatever one's political stance, I think most anyone would agree that Mrs. Reagan is a charming, gracious lady.

A number of years later, I had the pleasure of interviewing Maureen Reagan. Like Nancy, she was gracious and genuine, but I could see her father in her smile and in her charming manner of speaking.

Sally Field was as cute, bubbly, and vivacious as I expected. Our interview was during a movie junket in Chicago for *Norma Rae*. Sensing some apprehension on her part, I tried to put her at ease.

"If there's anything you don't want to talk about, we won't," I told her.

"Please don't ask me about Burt Reynolds," she implored.

So we talked about her movie, and then about her. As promised, I never mentioned Burt Reynolds, but she brought up the subject. She didn't call him Burt Reynolds, though. She always called him her boyfriend.

True star quality sometimes reveals itself in unexpected people.

Perhaps because of those pantyhose commercials, I thought I might not like Joe Namath. I interviewed him in Los Angeles, once again drawing the last time slot.

Stefanie Powers

A serious moment while interviewing Sally Field.

The minute I sat down, he won me over in thirty seconds. He turned out to be one of the warmest, nicest individuals I ever met. Who could resist that engaging smile and those adorable dimples!

Naturally, our conversation turned to football.

"I'm from Austin," I told him. "You have to say 'Hook 'em, Horns,'" I said, showing him the hand signal for the University of Texas football team.

He grabbed my hand, pulled it down, and said, "I can't do that."

"Why not?"

"Don't you know where I went to school?"

"Yes, but the people in Alabama won't watch this tape and the Texas folks will. If you don't give that sign, I'll be tarred and feathered."

At the end of the interview, he obliged me with a not too enthusiastic "Hook 'em, Horns" sign.

When we got off the air and were saying our good-byes, I told him, "I know you're tired and want to get out of here, but may I impose on you for a very special favor?"

He nodded his assent.

"You are very important to a couple of young people back home. One of them is my intern from UT who works with me at the TV station. She's madly in love with you.

"The other is my nephew, who idolizes you. He tries to walk and talk just like you. If I could have an autograph for those two, I'd be most grateful."

"Of course." He practically wrote both of them a letter. He was just precious. I thanked him profusely and started to leave.

He gently grabbed my arm and swung me around. "Wait a minute. Now may I ask a favor of you?"

"What is it?"

"You're such a neat lady. Could I kiss you good-bye?"

How could I resist that smile and those dimples? "Well, of course," I melted. "I thought you'd never ask!"

He kissed me on the cheek. I don't think I've washed that spot since!

Phyllis George was as beautiful, gracious, and articulate as one would expect a former Miss America to be. She came to Austin to be honored by the Headliners Club.

Before taping her interview, I asked if she would have any ob-

Phyllis George talks about her reign as Miss America.

*Phyllis George and Carolyn pose
for pictures for the crew.*

jections to recording the interview on a cassette to send to two young men in Knoxville, Tennessee, the nephews of dear friend and former roommate Julie Webb. Their sister was soon to compete in the Miss Tennessee pageant, so these young men were very interested in the Miss America pageant.

She taped the interview and afterward asked, "Is the tape still running? I'd like to say something special to those two boys.

"Hi, Cain, Hi, Bergen. What neat names you boys have. Hope I can meet you in person some day. Tell your sister when she competes in the pageant, just to be natural, be herself."

She continued the message for several minutes, making it very personalized.

I thanked her for taking time to be so thoughtful of two little boys, especially considering her tight schedule.

When they received the tape, Julie called to report on the excitement it caused.

"You probably heard them whooping and hollering all the way to Texas. They played it repeatedly for anyone who would listen, they were so proud of it," she said.

There's a special place in my heart for actor Tab Hunter. He came to Austin to perform at the Country Dinner Playhouse. The night before his first performance, my daughter Cindi called. She was teaching in Caldwell.

"Tomorrow night," she told me, "our National Honor Society is coming to the Country Dinner Playhouse. Andy, the son of my teaching aide, will be with them, and he has leukemia. He's a senior, president of the National Honor Society, and an athlete. Andy has never been to a play before and he's never met a star. Is there any way you could you get Tab Hunter's autograph for him?"

"I can't promise, but I'll do the best I can."

"Andy and his mom won't be disappointed if you can't, because they don't even know I'm asking."

The next day, before our interview, I said, "Tab, I have a big favor to ask. The National Honor Society is coming from Caldwell to see your play. Andy, the president of the society, is coming with them, and he has leukemia. He would like very much to get your autograph if possible.

"I don't know him, but my niece died of leukemia many years ago, so I understand what his family is going through. I remember many kindnesses extended to her and our family. If I could repay them to someone else, I'd be most grateful."

He looked at me, expressionless. "I'll take care of it," he assured me. I had no idea exactly what that meant.

Cindi called the next day and was so overcome with emotion she could hardly talk.

"Mother, you won't believe what happened." When Andy came in, very late, he woke everybody in his family.

"I just had the most exciting night of my life," he told them. "After the performance, Tab Hunter asked would Andy and his group from Caldwell stay for a few minutes. He and the cast came over and gave us autographs. He called me by name and made me feel we were friends."

When Andy's mom came to school that morning, relating the story with great excitement and gratitude, she told Cindi she had figured out how all this came to be.

With tears in her eyes she said, "I just want to thank you and your mom with all my heart."

When Cindi finished her story, we sobbed together on the phone.

Both Cindi and I wrote Tab Hunter a note to thank him for his kindness and compassion toward Andy, who died about three months later.

Send Me No Flowers is my favorite play, and it took on new dimensions when its star was Van Johnson at the Country Dinner Playhouse. He wasn't feeling well and was even running a fever when he came for the interview. It's unusual and commendable for an actor to honor an interview commitment when he is ill.

"Flowers are for the living. Isn't it terrible that we wait until someone dies to send them flowers," Mr. Johnson said during the interview. "But that's just the way we human beings are. Millions of dollars are spent in Hollywood when someone dies. I just wish we'd get into the habit of sending flowers while people are alive," he said.

We got through the interview, but he was so sick he could not perform that night or for the next three days. I sent flowers to his hotel. The card read, "Flowers are for the living. Thanks again for the delightful interview. Get well soon. Carolyn."

He was so appreciative that he took the time to come by the station and thank me personally for them.

Hubert Humphrey made a quick two-hour stop in Austin just for our interview. He was on his way to San Antonio, where he was scheduled to arrive before noon. The station arranged to tape him at 9:30 A.M., planning to play it during my show at noon.

As fate would have it, while I was en route to the station there was a terrible accident on Interstate-35 between Round Rock and Austin. Traffic backed up for miles and I was stuck, with no way to get off I-35. I was beside myself as my watch spun closer to 9:30 A.M. Unfortunately, there were no cell phones in those days.

My station news director knew about the wreck and alerted Mr. Kellam, who graciously greeted Mr. Humphrey. He told him he was sure I was stuck in the wreck traffic and that's why I wasn't there.

"We'll wait a few more minutes, because I know how important this interview is to her, but if she's not here soon, I'll have to let someone else do it," Mr. Kellam said.

I finally screeched into the parking lot about 9:40 A.M. Imagine the state I was in. I didn't even have time to check my makeup. I rushed into the studio and Hubert Humphrey put his arms around me.

"You poor dear, you must be a nervous wreck. Sit down and rest and have a cup of coffee. We can do the interview in a few minutes," he said.

I had done the unforgivable, been late for an interview. I couldn't believe his kindness, when I had delayed him. He realized, though, that I hadn't done it deliberately.

Since I wasn't part of the news department, I didn't have to talk about politics. We talked about family, about him, his wife, kids, and grandchildren. I had no preconceived ideas about him and really didn't have much feeling one way or the other. However, as I looked into his eyes, I thought he was one of the warmest, nicest human beings I had ever met. Why can't we see the real person like this in political campaigns?

My job afforded me the pleasure of interviewing many in the sports field—pro football players, basketball stars, skating champions, coaches, etc., but my interview with athlete Jesse Owens was truly a highlight of my life. He was so very special. He was born into a poor family, with skin the wrong color at that time in society. All the limitations were there, but he beat the odds and went all the way to the Olympics, representing a country that hadn't always supported him.

He became a champion, but Adolph Hitler refused to shake his hand because he was black. In spite of such incidents, he harbored no bitterness or resentment, only love for his fellow man. He spent most of his life helping others, especially young athletes.

Through tears, I looked at this kind, talented, capable man and asked if I might have the privilege of shaking his hand.

CHAPTER 5
CELEBRITIES BEHIND THE SCENES

Happiness adds and multiplies as we divide it with others.
—POSTER

The variety of celebrities I interviewed spiced up both my life and my show.

Justin Wilson, the Cajun cookbook author, was a hoot. He had so much natural wit and was so much fun that we spent most of his interview laughing.

When we finished, I thanked him for his time and reached over to shake his hand.

Grabbing me, he said, "Honey, where I come from, we don't shake hands with our women, we kiss 'em." And he planted a big smacker right on my lips.

Jimmy Dean was one of the best. He was so natural and quick on the draw. He muttered asides to the cameramen and at one point broke in and sang to me. What an entertainer!

Unfortunately, no one ever saw that show. It was taped on a Friday afternoon to be aired on Monday. On weekends, everyone at the station was totally immersed in football madness. Someone— no one ever admitted responsibility—grabbed my Jimmy Dean tape, clearly marked *Do Not Tape Over,* and taped the *Darrell Royal Show* on top of it, thus losing my interview forever.

One of my most emotional interviews was with Danny Thomas, the founder of St. Jude's Hospital for children in Memphis, Tennessee. He was very understanding and sympathetic when he learned my niece had died of leukemia and referred to my personal experience with the disease during his time with me.

That interview was done more by the interviewee than the interviewer.

"Don't worry, honey," he told me. "We'll make it through this." And he helped me do it.

When I interviewed Eileen Fulton, who had played Lisa for twenty years on *As the World Turns*, I expected her to be completely at ease. Wrong—she was a nervous wreck.

"Eileen, what's the matter?"

"I'm so nervous that I'm not sure I can do this. Everything I do is scripted and I memorize it. I'm not comfortable without a script," she moaned.

I told her to forget the cameras, look at me, and we'd talk as two friends would. I focused the conversation on unusual things that had happened during her career. As she recalled funny incidents, she began to relax and laugh.

After the interview she admitted, "That wasn't bad at all. In fact, it was fun."

Edgar Buchanan, who played Uncle Joe on *Petticoat Junction*, also was so nervous he broke into a cold sweat. He had the same problem as Eileen—he was uncomfortable sitting and chatting after being so accustomed to a scripted program.

I had found out from his biographical information that he was a dentist. He probably expected serious, probing questions about television and his career.

Instead, after introducing him to the viewers, I turned to him and said, "Edgar, I understand that before becoming an actor, you practiced dentistry." He looked surprised and a little off guard.

"I've really been having trouble with this tooth, could you take a look at it?" I joked. That cracked him up and he totally relaxed. The rest of the interview was smooth sailing.

After interviewing Ruta Lee several times, we became friends. She was starring in *Play It Again, Sam,* at the Country Dinner Playhouse in Austin. Chily and I decided to take our daughter Cindi and her husband, Mike, to the play to celebrate their first anniversary.

Knowing they were in the audience, Ruta sent them a note and invited us to join her backstage after the performance. When they met her, she had ordered a bottle of champagne to help them celebrate. A thoughtful, classy lady!

The unexpected made interviews fun.

For once, I had the first time slot when I interviewed Richard Pryor in New York for *Silver Streak*. This was usually an advantage because the stars are not tired out from repeatedly answering the same questions. This time, though, the early slot was no advantage at all.

My friend John Bustin, movie critic from Austin, warned me during the press conference that several other critics had angered Mr. Pryor, and he was so hot under the collar that he might be hostile unless I could soften him up.

While the crew was setting up the cameras and lights, I made it quite clear to Richard that it was my policy not to get into topics that might be awkward or embarrassing.

"Is there anything that you don't want to discuss?"

Looking at me hard as if he were evaluating my sincerity, he said very seriously, "Yes, please don't ask me about the day I raped the nun."

I gasped, and he began to laugh uproariously. "Just kidding."

I knew then that he trusted me, and we were going to have fun.

I always did my homework on the stars and studied the biographical information sent to me. And I liked to start off with something different or unexpected.

"Richard, I didn't know you were a basketball star in college," I began.

"I never was a basketball star."

"Oh, don't be bashful, I'm sure you were good."

"I know me, and I know I was never a basketball star," he insisted.

"But it says so right here in your press kit."

"Gimme that thing," he snapped, grabbing my information sheet. He read it, then demanded, "Who in the heck writes these things?"

I'm not sure I've ever forgiven Russ Tamblyn for the trick he played on me when I interviewed him when he was in Austin performing in St. Edward's University's summer theater program. I was interviewing him before an Austin High School student journalism group. I was anxious to make the interview special and show them exactly how it's done.

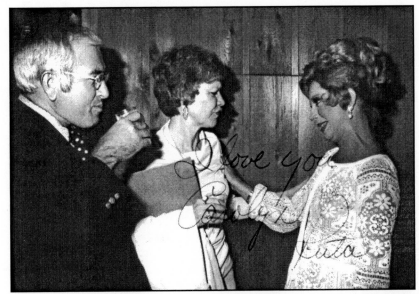

Ruta Lee welcomes Chily and Carolyn backstage at the Country Dinner Playhouse.

During an interview at New York's Plaza Hotel, Carolyn wonders what to expect next from comedian Richard Pryor.

Suddenly, he toppled over backward in his chair.

What should I do? Help him up? Call an ambulance? What? There he was, sprawled on the floor, but the director was laughing.

"Obviously, you didn't know I am an Olympic tumbling champion," he said to me.

As the kids roared, I accused, "You did that on purpose."

"Yeah, I just wanted to see what kind of reaction I'd get from you. I thought the kids would enjoy it," he said, doubling up with laughter.

I lucked out on a couple of interviews and did the right thing without even being aware of it. Star Trek's Leonard Nimoy said at the interview's conclusion, "Thank you so much."

"What did I do?"

"You're the first person who ever interviewed me without asking, 'Where are your ears?'"

I knew Steve Forrest was Dana Andrews' brother, but I never mentioned it during our interview.

"Thank you so much," he said. "I appreciate that you focused the interview on me and my accomplishments and not on the fact that I'm Dana Andrews' brother."

The same held true for Crystal Gayle.

"You made people see me as a singer in my own right and not just the sister of Loretta Lynn," was her comment.

I was dying to find out how much of J. R. Ewing was in Larry Hagman. I had plenty of opportunity to learn, because I got to escort him and his wife around a convention for about five days.

I had set up a press conference for 5:00 P.M. the first day so he could enjoy the rest of his stay.

"Please knock on my door at 4:45 P.M. so I'll know it's time for the press conference," he requested.

I knocked promptly at 4:45 P.M., he opened the door, and there he stood in his undershorts!

What's a lady to do? All I could think of to say was, "Where's your hat?"

Cracking up, he said, "Wait a minute, I'll get it." Jokester that he is, he had planned the whole scene just to shock me. It worked. He quickly put on his clothes, and we headed for the press conference. As I got to know him, I realized he's a very nice, sensitive, fun-loving person, not at all like J. R.

The ever-popular J. R. Ewing (Larry Hagman).

Larry Hagman talks about J. R. Ewing during a press conference at the St. Anthony Hotel in San Antonio.

When I took him to the airport, he took about ten envelopes from his pocket, gave them to me, and asked me to see that the addressees received them. He had written personal notes to people like the bartender, the maid, etc., and enclosed autographed pictures. I delivered them and everyone was tremendously pleased.

Bill Macy played Bea Arthur's husband on *Maude*.

I asked him, "Before you tape a show, what do you do to relax?"

"Glad you asked, because I do have a little routine. I find a corner, sit down, bow my head, and meditate. It really clears my mind. Want to see how it works? Close your eyes, be very, very quiet, and try not to think about anything."

Trying to do as he suggested, I suddenly got the giggles.

Coming out of his meditative state, Bill said, "What's so funny?"

"I had this mental picture of someone tuning in and seeing both of us sitting here as though we're asleep. That won't do much for my image as one who runs a lively show."

Brooke Shields was just a teenager when we met. Her movie *Tilt* never got off the ground, even though her acting was superb. She tried her best to be poised, but seemed uncomfortable talking about the movie. Her answers were "Yes, No, I guess so."

It dawned on me that we needed to talk about topics of greater interest to her—after all, she was a teenager. She began to smile, bubble, and act like a normal teen when I asked her how her room was decorated and if she kept it herself. She blossomed when she talked about her horses, cats, and her relationship with her mother.

My golfer husband was probably more excited than I about my interview with Arnold Palmer.

When I interviewed him on the golf course at Onion Creek, he gripped my hand so hard when he shook it that my butterfly ring scratched his hand. He drew back his hand and rubbed it. With horror, I realized what had happened.

"Oh, I'm so sorry," I apologized profusely.

"That's OK, but if I damage my grip today and lose this golf match, it's going to be all that butterfly's fault," he said with a grin.

Fortunately, he won, so the butterfly and I were off the hook—at least with Arnold Palmer.

Not so with my husband. "How dare you scratch Arnold Palmer's hand?" Chily was mortified.

Jane Pauley came across like the traditional girl next door. She had just taken over the *Today* show, and critics sniped that she was trying unsuccessfully to be another Barbara Walters. But I thoroughly enjoyed interviewing her and found her to be sincere and down to earth. I'm glad she has proved to the critics that she has a very successful style all her own.

I expected Bill Murray to be hilarious, but he was very serious. He told me that if he had not become an actor, he had wanted to be a doctor.

"Why?"

"Because I've always wanted to heal people."

"Bill, in a way you do. Laughter is very therapeutic, you know."

"I'd never thought about that. I hope you're right," he told me.

A junket to California for the promotion of *Star Wars* was a real extravaganza. We media people basked in the red-carpet treatment we received. Not only were we entertained royally, but we could interview the stars—Mark Hamil, Carrie Fisher, Harrison Ford, etc., right on the sets where the movie was filmed.

Carrie Fisher and Mark Hamil were light-hearted and fun to be with. Harrison Ford, though, was intense and difficult to reach. We all knew *Star Wars* would be an all-time classic, but we didn't real-

Carrie Fisher shares a humorous story about Star Wars.

Carolyn concentrates during an interview with Harrison Ford in Los Angeles.

Mark Hamil and Carolyn chat on the set of Star Wars *in Los Angeles.*

ize it would make a comeback twenty years later and be a big hit for another generation.

Woody Allen was different, to say the least. I had a 4:00 P.M. appointment to interview Woody in New York. With several hours to kill, I decided to go shopping. I got caught in a torrential downpour and there was no cab in sight. Time was running out, and cabs always disappear in the rain, so I caught a bus.

In the process, I got drenched and barely made it back to the hotel five minutes before interview time. There was no time to freshen up, so I went to the interview soaking wet, with my hair straggling in my face, looking like a drowned Big Apple rat.

I apologized to Woody for my looks, but he was very gracious and said, "You look lovely. I wish I could look that good when I'm soaking wet."

Throughout the interview, I sensed insecurity in Woody, almost as if he thought of himself as a loser. I looked like such a bedraggled loser, I guess he considered us soul mates. I believe my drenched state actually enhanced the interview. We never know when a calamity can turn into a blessing.

Perhaps one of the most nervous stars I ever interviewed was John Belushi. Fortunately, something went wrong with the camera and we had a chance to chat before we taped the interview.

Commenting on my rings he said, "Even wearing jewelry makes me nervous. I don't know why."

"John, do I make you nervous?"

"This whole scene makes me nervous," he replied. "I like you, though."

"I hope you can relax and we can just have fun," I tried to reassure him.

We had a pleasant session, but he never got completely comfortable.

There were some interviews I could have done without.

I interviewed Jill Clayburgh twice, once in New York and once in Dallas.

The first one was bad and the second one was worse. She wouldn't do an interview without her producer. She was uncooperative and curt during both the interviews. I thought perhaps we had a personality conflict, but other media people had the same problem with her.

After viewing the interview tape, Dana, my director, didn't want to air it.

"That's really bad," he said.

"Who's bad?"

"She is."

"My viewers know me well enough to realize I tried to get a good interview," I declared.

We aired the tape and the switchboard lit up with callers demanding to know why she was being so ugly to me.

"She's secure on the screen, being someone else, but not comfortable being Jill Clayburgh," one of my colleagues summed up her behavior.

Richard Dreyfuss was nice to me, but our interview was only so-so. He seemed so cold. And my estimation of him plummeted when he refused to autograph a picture for a fellow interviewer to give to her two small sons, who were ardent fans of his.

"I don't give autographs. I never have and I don't plan to start now," he haughtily told her.

Although I interviewed hundreds of stars during my career, I had no strong feelings about the personalities of many of them. Others provided me memorable stories, some of which I've shared with you.

There were a few who made instant impressions on me. Whether my intuition was valid or invalid—here are my vibes:

Erik Estrada—a big Teddy bear;

Ann-Margret—an amazing depth not always detected on screen;

Cybill Shepherd and Susan Sarandon—two of a kind—seemed shallow;

Myron Floren—not only a talented musician, but a warm, caring individual;

Kate Jackson—the kind of person I'd like for a friend;

Jane Fonda—struck me as rude and overbearing;

Henry "The Fonz" Winkler— adorable;

Michael Douglas—serious, but easy to talk to;

Beau Bridges—a bundle of fun;

Jack Lemmon—truly a legend—a class act;

Tennessee Ernie Ford—a dear, lovable person. I wanted to hug him; and

Nick Nolte—charming—what a smile.

Susan Sarandon.

Beau Bridges delights Carolyn while describing his love for Texas.

* * *

Receiving a letter from the late Madalyn Murray O'Hair was the last thing I ever expected. But there it was on my desk. I ripped it open, anxious to see what she could possibly have to say to me.

Something inside me signaled that it was not a fan letter. My intuition was right on target.

Ms. O'Hair was demanding—not requesting—equal time on my program to counteract a show in which I featured three young Christian boys who shared their experiences at a Campus Crusade youth camp in California.

Her very intimidating letter claimed that, as an atheist, she had the right to an equal amount of airtime discussing atheism.

I took the letter to Mr. Kellam for direction on how to handle it.

"Don't worry about it, Mrs. Jackson. I'll take care of it," he assured me.

His short, businesslike reply politely thanked her for her interest in the show, but firmly informed her that the program I did on Campus Crusade represented the efforts and interests of thousands of people and that anytime she had something of that magnitude to present, we would consider her request.

Until that time, best regards, or in other words, "Get lost!"

I always tried to treat my guests with the utmost respect, but sometimes it was hard to do.

Putting microphones on guests, both men and women, always was done either by the floor manager or one of the cameramen. This was to ensure the mike was secure and in the right place. Also, it was a courtesy to the guests, and most appreciated the assistance.

But not Gloria Steinem. As the cameraman approached her with the mike, she jerked it out of his hand.

"I'm quite capable of doing that myself," she snapped.

Is that what the feminist movement is all about? I wondered.

I couldn't resist the temptation to counteract her rudeness. I turned to Ted and smiled.

"Ted, would you please help me with my mike?"

With a wink, he replied, "I'd be happy to."

I enjoy being treated like a lady.

CHAPTER 6
MAGIC MOMENTS

Friends are the daisies in the garden of life.
—CHRISTIAN POSTER

There were no Orientals in the area where I grew up. My first experience with them came as a result of my TV show.

I decided to do a program on the Chinese New Year—to explore its origin, significance, and celebrations. A friend told me about Mr. and Mrs. Harry Ng, who owned a Chinese restaurant in South Austin.

I contacted them and invited them to be guests on my show, and they graciously accepted.

The day of their appearance, they arrived laden with Chinese food for the entire crew and an assortment of gifts for me. Their generosity overwhelmed me.

The show was so successful that we made it an annual affair that endured the entire time I was on TV.

Best of all, I developed a meaningful and lasting friendship with the Ngs. Shortly after our first broadcast, the Ngs invited Chily and me to join them and some of their friends for a private Chinese New Year's dinner at their restaurant.

What a surprise when we arrived to find that all the guests were their American friends—their doctor, their dentist, loyal patrons of their restaurant, etc.

The dinner was their way of saying thanks to a circle of Americans who had become their friends.

It was an unforgettable, beautiful evening filled with unsurpassed graciousness and hospitality.

I sent them a small plant as a token of my appreciation for being included in the event. Two weeks later I received a box of gifts and food from them as a token of their appreciation for my friendship.

Never have I encountered more generous, appreciative, caring people. Whatever I did for them, they returned threefold. How grateful I am that TV brought them into my life, and what a warm feeling for the Oriental people they instilled in me!

* * *

Among my most cherished treasures are the books that were autographed by the authors I've interviewed. Reading always has been an integral part of my life—bringing knowledge and a world of adventure to me.

Because of my love of books, meeting many famous authors was a special privilege.

Many times I stayed up until the wee hours finishing a book in preparation for the next day's interview. I would not consider doing an interview without having read the entire book. Anything less would have been an insult to the author.

After one interview with an author, President Johnson's younger daughter, Luci, called to compliment me on my knowledge of the book.

"I think it's degrading for an interviewer to talk with an author without bothering to read the book. It was obvious that you have read the book. Thank you for being so professional," she said.

Although each author touched my life in a unique way, there was one whom I seemed destined to meet.

While browsing through a bookstore one day, I spotted a book entitled *I've Got to Talk to Somebody, God.* Just the title made me buy it.

It was a book of prayers by Marjorie Holmes. But these were not your ordinary prayers. They were prayers a woman might whisper to God while ironing, washing the dishes, or performing any of the other routine tasks women do.

Harry and Lee Ng celebrate the Chinese New Year on The Carolyn Jackson Show.

Chatting with Luci Johnson.

Each prayer seemed to fit me perfectly, as though Mrs. Holmes had been reading my mind and knew how to express my feelings to God. I kept the book always close at hand and referred to the prayers over and over again.

Often the thought crossed my mind—what a joy it would be to meet this woman, Marjorie Holmes, to whom I felt so close.

One day as I was leaving the station, the receptionist stopped me.

"You have a call. Want to take it, or shall I get a number and you can call her back tomorrow?"

"I'll take it. Hello?"

"Hello, Carolyn. This is Marjorie Holmes."

"Wha-, what did you say?"

"This is Marjorie Holmes."

"*The* Marjorie Holmes?" Melodious laughter filled the phone.

"Well, I'm the only one I know. Carolyn, are you familiar with my books?"

"Oh, YES."

"Good. Well, I'm on vacation visiting relatives in Lampasas. They are big fans of yours. They insisted I call and see if perhaps you'd like to interview me while I'm here."

"Yes, yes, yes, I'd love to." At this point I was trembling with excitement and silently whispering, "Thank you, Lord."

We set up the interview date, and I anxiously awaited her arrival in the lobby. At first glance, I knew she was everything I expected her to be—vivacious, animated, very feminine, and radiating an inner beauty.

What surprised me was her tiny size—like a precious fairy god-mother.

Our interview was sheer delight. The special bonus was that following the show, all her books in every bookstore in Austin sold out, with many going on the waiting list for reorders.

Although her publishing company had never before included Austin on her book tour, they did from that moment on. With each future release of a new book, Marjorie again appeared with me on TV. Each time, all her books sold out.

My admiration for Marjorie and our friendship grew deeper with each passing year. She touched my life more than she'll ever know.

God bless you, Marjorie Holmes.

* * *

Driving to work one cool, crisp April day, my thoughts were racing ahead to the evening when we'd have a family get-together to celebrate my birthday.

When I arrived at the station, a few people greeted me with a cheery "Happy Birthday," and there were several cards waiting for me on my desk.

Dana, my director, walked into my office to discuss the show, but didn't mention my birthday—nor was there a card from him. I must admit I was a little hurt, but I reminded myself that guys aren't sentimental about those things like girls are. So I quickly put my birthday out of my mind.

The show went smoothly, the guest was interesting, but the time seemed to pass more quickly than usual. Mary Strickland, my floor manager, gave me the wrap sign, and I began to thank my guest and say my good-byes.

Instead of the theme song playing as the closing credits rolled, the camera stayed focused on me and I heard a familiar voice (Dana's) saying, "Ladies and gentlemen, Carolyn thinks this program is over, but it isn't. We tricked her with our time cues. In the remaining few minutes, we'd like to present this tribute to Carolyn as our way of saying happy birthday." With that, a montage of pictures of my face with various expressions appeared on the screen with the background music, "I've Grown Accustomed to Her Face." A small insert in the upper right-hand corner showed me watching the screen with tears rolling down my face.

Suddenly, Dana's strange antics during the past week made sense. He claimed he'd bought a new camera and was practicing using it. Every time I looked up, he'd be standing there with his camera saying, "smile," or "look sad" or "look mad" or "look silly" or "make a face at me." He made it seem like a game, and I fell right into his trap, all under the guise of helping him perfect his photography skills.

It dawned on me his aim had been to put together a lovely birthday tribute to me. Dana walked out of the control room with a twinkle in his eye and a sheepish grin and gave me a big hug. As the show ended, all the crew and many staff members gathered in the studio to sing "Happy Birthday."

Once again, I was reminded how fortunate I was to have such a terrific director and such a precious friend.

The crew and friends throw a surprise birthday party for Carolyn on her show's set.

* * *

All of Austin was excited about the ice rink that would be a part of the new Northcross Mall. This was a first for our city. Little did I dream it would become an important part of my life and my show.

As the grand opening of the rink approached, I was summoned to a meeting with Gus Stewart, our local sales manager, and Bud and Shirley Ayers. Bud was the manager of the rink, and Shirley, his wife and a professional skater, was the instructor.

They presented a unique idea to me. Shirley wanted to teach me how to skate. The station would film my first lesson, another about six months later, and one after a year. These would be featured on my show, and I'd keep viewers informed of my progress between films. We would both benefit. They would get advertising for the new rink, and we would get some exclusive programming.

Of course I said yes and couldn't wait to get home to share my excitement and enthusiasm with my family. The girls thought it was a super idea, but Chily looked at me as if I had just fallen off a turnip truck.

"Are you crazy? You in your forties are going to take up ice skating? And let them film you making a fool of yourself? What if you break your leg—that'll be terrific advertising for them!" he bellowed.

Being the stubborn Taurus that I am, I became more determined than ever after he waved that red flag in my face. Seeing that "I'll do it or die trying" look in my eye, he mellowed somewhat, saying, "It's your legs—do whatever you want to. And I'll try not to say I told you so."

The first lesson was a hoot. As one might expect, I was stiff, shaky, and scared. Shirley spent nearly all the first lesson teaching me how to fall.

"Everyone falls," she reassured me. "But you must learn how to do it without injuring yourself."

The response to the airing of my first lesson was overwhelming. The viewers loved it and expressed great interest in following my progress. Many were even inspired to give it a try themselves.

Daughter Carol took lessons with me to give me moral support. It was disgusting how quickly she caught on and how I had to struggle! Could that have been attributed to the difference in our ages?

Although I took only one lesson per week, I found myself slipping away to the rink to practice at least three or four times a week. I was totally hooked on the sport and found it to be one of the most enjoyable activities I had ever tried.

Often a viewer approached me at the rink to offer words of encouragement and praise. Music to my ears!

After the airing of the second film, viewers again called in their approval of the segment and expressed amazement and enthusiasm at my skating ability. Even skeptical Chily was so impressed that he bought me my very own ice skates for Christmas.

The final segment aired exactly a year after I first ventured timidly onto the ice. I'm proud to report I performed a dance on the ice with a male partner.

Who says you can't teach an old dog, er . . . TV personality, new tricks?

* * *

We all have our "down days." Fortunately, I didn't have many, but when I had one, it was a lulu. I could really put on a pity party when things seemed out of whack. But God always sent someone to lift my spirits—usually a child. Two such occasions are indelible in my mind.

One day as I left the station, I decided to stop in a nearby grocery store and do my shopping on the way home. I was tired, and grocery shopping was the last thing I wanted to do, but it's one of those chores required of moms.

As I scurried down the aisle filling my basket, I brooded—not only did I have to buy this stuff, but then I had to go home and cook it. No doubt my face reflected "Poor Pitiful Pearl" when out of nowhere a little black girl approached me.

With a big smile she asked, "Are you that lady on TV?"

"Well, I'm one of them."

"Do you happen to have any of those autographs?"

"I bet I could find one," I said as I searched my purse for a piece of paper and a pen. I asked her name, then wrote her a little note.

When I handed it to her, her little face beamed. She stretched out her arms to me, and as I bent over, she gave me a big hug and kiss. I can still see her angelic little face.

The blues were gone and grocery shopping suddenly was fun.

＊ ＊ ＊

Herb Hansen, one of the salesmen at KTBC, was one of my favorite people. His incomparable sense of humor, positive attitude, and upbeat style made him a ray of sunshine.

His son (a chip off the old block) pulled me out of the doldrums another day.

I was sitting at my desk in a gloomy mood when in walked Herb. Just seeing his cheerful face lifted my spirits, but then he handed me a surprise. It was a poster his son had painstakingly drawn for me.

Done in minute detail, it pictured me on my TV set. In big bold letters, it proclaimed, *The Carolyn Jackson Show*. I couldn't have been more pleased if he had handed me a Picasso.

As I sat there admiring my prize possession, I thought, "If you have the love and admiration of a child, nothing else in the world matters."

CHAPTER 7

OUTTAKES

Humor is the harmony of the heart.
—DOUGLAS JERROLD

Live TV is wonderful, but tricky. No matter what happens, you have to keep going and roll with the punches. On tape, mistakes can be erased and the show made to look good. Live, what you see is what you get, and you have to make the best of it.

Television is nothing without commercials. One of my show's sponsors was PAM, the cooking spray, and I did their commercials live. I would introduce my show and the day's guest, then do the live commercial, and then cut to news director Joe Roddy for headline news.

Joe and I sat very close together at a table. During my commercial, I was supposed to pick up a pan and say, "When you pick up a pan, spray it with PAM," and then do it.

One day the camera crew played a trick on me. Without my knowledge, they fixed the nozzle on the PAM can so it would point at Joe's face instead of the pan. When I sprayed, PAM spewed all over his face and nose.

He started to sputter and cough and coughed and coughed and coughed. He'd gasp a few words of the news, then cough some more. Fortunately, the audience couldn't see that I was doubled up with laughter.

Joe didn't think it was so funny. I finally convinced him I had nothing to do with the direction of the spray, and in time he forgave me.

Then there was the Gage Furniture commercial. One day Monica Davis of the continuity department rushed into the studio just before airtime, waving a piece of paper.

"Gage Furniture wants to run a commercial in the break just before your show. You have to do it right this second," Monica said.

"Monica, I haven't seen the copy."

"Oh, you know you can do it. Don't worry about it, just do it."

"OK," I agreed, positioning myself in front of the camera. Mind you, this was supposedly live, and I hadn't seen the copy. Imagine the expression on my face as I read on the TelePrompTer:

"This week at Gage, save nine cents on any sofa or chair by anyone. That's right, find cheap used furniture nobody else wants. This is Gage's sale of sales. Take your choice of old fabrics, torn velvets, or broken brocades. Gage's sale of sales is going on right now at all six Gage stores.

"April Fool!"

I had totally forgotten it was April Fool's Day. I looked up to see nearly everyone in the studio roaring with laughter. Thank goodness it didn't go out over the air, or I'm sure Gage would have sued us for all we were worth.

Karavel Shoes commercials were always live. The day's featured shoes appeared on the monitor while I read the script from the TelePrompTer. One day the monitor was there, but it had been turned around so my guest couldn't see it. So neither could I see the shoes when I did my commercial.

When time came for the commercial, the cameraman must have been in "la la land," because he failed to turn on the TelePrompTer. I made up the commercial as I went along about how beautiful and comfortable the shoes were. All the while, I prayed I wasn't describing evening slippers while the monitor displayed tennis shoes.

Another day, those shoes proved to be more than comfortable. The news girl and I were sitting on the steps on my set waiting to begin, and she was holding a pair of the shoes. Suddenly, a studio light popped, sparks flew, and the carpet caught fire. She quickly beat out the flames with the Karavel shoes.

In my commercial, as I raved on about their comfort and style, I bit my tongue to keep from adding, "And man, can they put out fires!"

Every other Tuesday I had a cooking segment on my show. Two women from Southern Union Gas came to help. They always brought a finished product so the viewers could see how the dish was supposed to look, then they put the ingredients together during the segment.

One day the dish was muffins, and they came to the set in a cute little basket, which was put into the oven. Someone accidentally turned the oven up very high, and we suddenly noticed smoke pouring out as the muffins and their basket merrily burned up.

About that time, my helper, Jenny, said "Now, let's take a look at our finished muffins."

"Jenny, I'm afraid our muffins are very well done," I said, opening the oven door and displaying the pitiful burned-up basket and the blackened muffins.

I assured the viewers that before our fire the muffins looked beautiful.

* * *

On television you have to be ready. No dead time is allowed. One day I had a memory expert from UT as my guest. I asked him why I could remember well who sat next to me in second grade, but sometimes could not recall what I did yesterday at 3:00 P.M.

"Oh, there's a very simple explanation," he said, and launched into it. Except it wasn't all that simple. In fact, it was very technical, and I tried very hard to understand and concentrate on what he was saying.

In fact, I tried so hard, I committed TV's worst no-no. I got so intense and involved that I failed to think ahead. Suddenly, my guest stopped talking, and I went totally blank. Zilch. Brain fade.

I sat there for what seemed like an eternity, but it probably was just a few seconds. My expression told him something was amiss.

"Is something wrong?"

I decided honesty was the best policy. "Would you believe, I can't remember what my next question was going to be," I stammered.

"Well, this is why that happens," he said, and began another explanation while I regained my composure.

It came off so sincerely and spontaneously, everyone thought we had planned it.

My set at KTBC was very open, and one day that caused a problem. I had a new news girl, Barbara Monaco. She was cutting her TV teeth by practicing headline bits on my show before moving to the 6:00 P.M. news.

Barbara and I were sitting on the steps in front of my set's fake window just thirty seconds before going on the air live. We already had our standby notice.

Suddenly, a voice said, "I ain't never seen no live TV show before." Turning, I saw a face in the window that looked like Mortimer Snerd. A guy in overalls, soda can in hand, stuck his head through the window.

I thought it was a prank planned by the crew, so I went along. "Oh, you haven't seen a live TV show before. Well, welcome, you're about to see one now," I said brightly.

I noticed that Mary Strickland, our floor manager, had put down her headset. Both cameramen looked like ghosts. Then I heard the director bellowing from the control room, "Who the hell is that?"

Suddenly, I knew this was no joke, that this guy was for real. But who was he?

About that time, Mary grabbed him by the overalls from behind and yanked him out of the window just before the cameras rolled. I came on, big smile, very happy.

"Welcome to the show." I mentioned our guest's name, then announced, "But first, here's Barbara Monaco with today's headlines."

I looked at Barb and she was frozen in place. Never having seen anything like this chaotic situation, she didn't have a clue what to do.

"Actually, we're going to take a short break, but we'll be back with Barb and the news in just a few moments," I said.

We thawed out Barb and got through the show. Then we learned the intruder had just gotten out of prison and stepped off a bus across the street from KTBC. He headed over, came in, and told the receptionist he was looking for a job.

He asked to use the restroom, and she directed him to the second floor. He saw the studio sign and just wandered in. He stepped behind the flaps and voilà! He was on my set.

* * *

You haven't experienced live TV until you have a chimp on your show.

One of my guests was a very well-trained female chimp—accompanied by her trainer. The chimp had been in lots of movies and was accustomed to attention. She had on a cute little outfit, complete with full skirt and bonnet. When I tried to talk to her, she hid behind her trainer like a child.

The trainer said, "Ignore her until she gets used to you and the situation."

So I talked to the trainer, asking her how she trained the chimp and in which movies the chimp had starred, etc.

The chimp realized I was ignoring her, so she patted my arm and then my leg, trying to get my attention. The segment was just about over, so I told the chimp how much I'd enjoyed having her on my show.

She jumped into my lap, threw her arms around me, and smacked me right on my lips.

For another show, I scheduled the president of the Goat Raisers Association to come in and talk about raising goats, what they did, etc.

The day he came, I was on vacation. I had asked him to come to the studio at 11:00 A.M. to talk, then go on into the studio at noon and do the show.

I had expected two people, and no one had mentioned bringing any goats. Not only did they bring a couple of goats, they arrived at 9:00 A.M.

Need I tell you, with two goats running around KTBC from 9:00 A.M. to noon, there was poo-poo everywhere—in the coffee shop, in the halls. Everywhere! When I returned from my vacation, there was a sign on my office door that said, "Poo-poo to you, too." And my director wouldn't even speak to me for several days.

"I know you did it on purpose. You did it to get even with me for everything I have ever done to you," he accused.

"I promise, I had no idea they were bringing the goats," I vowed.

The staff was convinced I had planned to have a couple of goats come to try to wreck KTBC, before I skipped out on vacation. Now, would I do a thing like that?

When the circus came to Austin, several elephants lumbered along in the parade that strutted down Congress Avenue.

My director got the bright idea that I should start my show out by the big studio door and then let an elephant carry me onto the set. Me, let an elephant wrap his trunk around my waist and carry me onto the set on live television? Never! But I did it, and it was fun.

Goats and poo-poo and circus elephants I could survive, but I admit I was nervous when my guest was a full-grown lion.

"Are you sure this lion is tame?" I asked his trainer.

"There's no such thing as a tame lion. Trained, but not tame. But don't worry, he really likes girls," the trainer said.

"As friends or food?" I quavered.

"Don't worry, you'll be fine," the trainer assured me.

I'm sure the viewers were aware how scared I was. I wasn't used to standing about a foot away from such a huge lion. But he just roared a couple of times as his trainer chatted with me, and it turned out to be a good show.

Six weeks later, my friendly lion was in Florida promoting a shopping mall. Something spooked him, and he mauled a TV personality's arm. I counted my blessings.

Area football rivalry even invaded my set.

Paul Alexander, one of our personable young newsmen, had been a football star in nearby Lockhart, Texas, when he was in high school. I was a strong supporter of my hometown Taylor Ducks.

When Lockhart and Taylor were to lock horns on the gridiron, Paul and I made a friendly bet on the game's outcome. If his Lockhart Lions won, I would have to sing the Lockhart alma mater live on my show. If my Ducks won, he would sing Taylor's alma mater.

Taylor won, but it was a mixed blessing. First I had to teach Paul the song, which was not easy to sing. And singing was not one of his talents. But true to his word, he sang the Taylor alma mater live, and the viewers were delighted with his good humor and sportsmanship.

* * *

Practical jokes were a way of life with Austin's "Head Honcho of Humor," Cactus Pryor. Cactus was program director at KTBC, and he had plenty of fun at my expense.

Humorist Art Buchwald was in Austin to deliver a speech and was to be the guest on my show. He was to arrive about noon, meaning he would reach the studio after I was already on the air, and I wouldn't have a chance to chat with him before we went on.

When I walked into the studio, Cactus was there. Following my show, he was going to do a radio interview with Art.

Cactus pulled me to the side and warned me I'd better pronounce Art's last name correctly, or he'd be really mad.

"Don't you pronounce it Art Buck-wald?" I asked, doubtfully.

"No, no, no. It's Art Butt-wald," Cactus insisted.

"Butt-wald?"

"I know Buchwald's the way it's spelled, but I've met him and that's not the way he pronounces it. He gets really paranoid if you mispronounce it," Cactus deadpanned.

I fell for it hook, line, and sinker. I sat down in front of the camera and Cactus never changed his expression. Fifteen seconds before airtime, Cactus repented and yelled at me, "I was just kidding, it's Art Buck-wald!"

The next second, the red light came on and I was on the air. I shudder to think how humiliated I would have been if I'd had this renowned gentleman on the air and introduced him as Art Butt-wald.

One day I entered my office, went over to my desk, and pulled out my chair. To my horror, there was a body curled up under my desk. I screamed at the top of my lungs, but it was just Cactus, who claimed to be taking a nap.

Another time I was on the air live, sitting at my table while the

Cactus Pryor and Carolyn share an interview with Cathy Rigby.

camera zoomed in for a close shot. Cactus crawled under the table
and kept hitting my knee with a ruler where the doctor taps it to
check your reflexes.

I still wonder what the audience thought as I helplessly jerked
and jerked and jerked.

* * *

In his book *Talk of Texas,* Jack Maguire spins a tale that gives me
the shivers. He tells about a Texas television station that holds some
kind of record for long-distance and long-lasting transmission. In
September 1953, TV screens in many parts of England suddenly
began projecting the call letters of TV station KLEE in Houston. It
was such a unique phenomenon that some viewers took photos of
the image.

But that's only half the story. KLEE went off the air in 1950,
three years before its signal was picked up in England.

When I read that, I absolutely shuddered. That says to me that
all the goofs and mistakes I've made are somewhere out there in the
universe, just hanging around. Someday, when my great-great-
grandchildren are watching TV, I'll pop up on the screen with one
of those mistakes. And they'll shriek, "Oh, look, there's Mimi
again!"

CHAPTER 8
TILT

We do not remember days—we remember moments.
—CHRISTIAN POSTER

My life on television led me into some life-changing situations. One incident that befell me while in Los Angeles brought me a new appreciation of the life I shared with my loved ones.

The station would send me out in the summer before the new fall TV series started to interview the stars for the new series. I'd do about ten interviews in one day. It was a time in my life when everything seemed to be so fast-paced, so hectic and chaotic. I think I was just rushing and pushing too much. I packed very rapidly that day and didn't even say good-bye to anyone. I certainly didn't tell anyone I loved them—I just left.

I reached Los Angeles about 5:00 P.M. and went to the hotel. A reception was planned for that evening to give the media people our instructions and orientation and let us meet one another. Then the interviews were to be conducted the next day.

I stayed at the reception until about 10:00 P.M., enjoying visiting with everyone, and then decided it was time to return to my room and get a good night's rest so I would be ready for the next day's interviews.

I was on about the twentieth floor in a hotel in Burbank. I

boarded the elevator with two small children, a little girl and a little boy, probably about five and eight years old. I wondered why they were in the elevator alone at that hour of the night, but I just smiled at them and spoke as the elevator started down.

Suddenly, it stopped. We expected the door to open and someone to get on, but that didn't happen. Then the elevator's lights went out.

This was very frightening, and I realized something definitely was wrong. A tiny bit of light was showing at the top, so I looked for a telephone, but there was none. Then I pressed the alarm button repeatedly, but nothing happened.

I tried to stay calm because of the children, but I was quite frightened. Was the hotel on fire? Had there been an earthquake? Why didn't someone respond to the alarm? I kept pressing the button, but no one came.

I could tell the children were getting very, very frightened. I knew I had to calm them down.

I said, "Why don't we just sit down? Someone will come get us in a minute." So we sat down, and I learned the children were from Missouri. Their parents were downstairs in the cabaña, and they just wanted to ride up and down in the elevator for a while, then go back to their room.

I told them about Texas and we chatted, and time went on and on. Periodically, I got up and pushed the alarm button, but nothing happened.

Suddenly, the little girl said, "I'm having a hard time breathing."

I replied, "You're just a little scared—you'll be all right." But then I realized I wasn't breathing so well myself. I wondered, "Is this elevator airtight? Are we going to use up all the oxygen?"

For the first time in my life, I realized that I could die. I'd never had that thought before.

I thought, "Life is kind of like a pinball machine. You play the game and you push and push and you shove, then all of a sudden you shove a little bit too hard and the thing lights up and in great big letters says, 'Tilt.'"

My mind spun like that pinball machine. I thought to myself, "That's what I've been doing. I've been pushing so hard and all of a sudden, here's the signal that says, 'Slow down, kid.'"

The thought crossed my mind that if I were going to die, how

I wished I had taken a little bit more time that morning to say good-bye.

I longed for one more chance to say "I love you" to my husband, to my daughters, to my parents. I thought, "If I can get out of here, I just want to tell them I love them."

Finally, the little girl became nearly hysterical, and we tried to open the door. We forced the inner one completely open, but could only get the other door open a few inches. I could see we were stuck between floors, but apparently no major disaster had occurred.

Why no one had responded to the alarm, I don't know, but I stuck my mouth to that crack and screamed at the top of my lungs. I screamed again, and finally two delightful young men from Australia, guests at the hotel, showed up. No knights in shining armor could have been more welcome!

"We heard you, but couldn't figure out what floor you were on. Hang on, we're going to get you out of there," they assured us.

They found a stick and used it as a crowbar to force the outer door open wider. They rescued the kids first, then said, "Now you."

"Do you really think I can squeeze through that tiny space?"

"Sure, just turn sideways."

They must have seen the horror on my face because one of them was so cute. He leaned down and said, "That sure is a pretty hairdo."

That broke the spell. I relaxed, and they managed to pull me through that crack. We'd been stuck in that elevator for an hour and a half.

When I finally got out, I looked around for the children, but they were gone. I don't know where they evaporated to, because I was going to take them downstairs to their parents and explain what had happened. I guess they were so scared that they just dashed down the stairs.

I thanked the two gentlemen repeatedly, but could not bring myself to enter another elevator. I took the stairs and must have walked down six or seven flights, but no way was I going to get back in an elevator.

By the time I reached my room, I was hysterical. I cried and cried, but finally said to myself, "Take a shower and get over this." By the time I got to bed, it was about 1:00 A.M., and I had to get up bright and early that morning, looking refreshed for the interviews.

I made it through the day, and on the flight home everything looked so beautiful. The sky and clouds and everything seemed to take on new beauty and meaning. It was if I were seeing the world for the first time.

When I landed in Austin, I got in the car and started to drive home. How many thousands of times I had made that trip between Austin and Taylor, but everything seemed so different. Everything looked exquisite! I saw things like cows romping in the pasture that I had never noticed before. You would have thought I had never made that drive before in my life. It was like I had been blind and was suddenly blessed with sight.

By the time I reached home, I was crying. I ran into the house and Chily was waiting for me. I threw my arms around him, blubbering, "I love you, I love you, I love you!"

Backing away, he said, "Well, it certainly seems painful."

When I explained what had happened, both of us rejoiced that I was safely home. I told my story repeatedly to family and friends, hardly able to contain my joy at being delivered from possible serious injury or death. I thanked the Lord that He had spared my life, allowing me more time with my precious family.

* * *

One Sunday, I read in the *Austin American-Statesman* about the Heimlich method of saving choking victims. The article was very interesting, and I read it several times. I was so impressed that I cut it out and put it in the drawer. I didn't know why, but I felt it was necessary to keep this article.

While I was visiting my parents that afternoon, my mother told me about a cousin in Dallas who had been eating in a restaurant and choked on chicken salad. The owner had been trained in the Heimlich method, and he rescued her. He broke her ribs, but he saved her life.

What a strange coincidence that I saw the article that morning, then my mother shared my cousin's experience that afternoon.

In the evening friends called, and in the course of conversation they told me about a friend of theirs who had choked on steak in a restaurant and a friend saved his life using the Heimlich method.

I said to myself, "Wait a minute, there's a message coming

through here. I'm not sure exactly what, but, God, what are you trying to tell me?"

I didn't sleep well and got up with the strong impression I had to do a show on the Heimlich method right away.

That was almost impossible, because shows were scheduled for as much as six weeks in advance. I knew I didn't have an opening for at least that long. But I still felt such an urgency; I was almost paranoid about it.

When I got to my office the next day, I was looking at the calendar trying to decide who I could reschedule when the phone rang with a cancellation for the next day. Immediately, I called the fire department and asked if they were trained in saving people from choking using the Heimlich method.

"Yes, ma'am, we are."

"Well, would it be possible for you to send somebody over to demonstrate that method on my television show tomorrow? I realize this is very short notice and I apologize, but I just had a cancellation and I have a real urgency about putting this on TV right away."

"We'll be most happy to accommodate you. We'll be there."

On the air, the firefighters explained the method very thoroughly and demonstrated it on each other.

Then one said to me, "Now you must try it."

"That's a great idea. I want to show everybody that anyone can do this."

The firefighter placed my hands just right and made me perform the maneuver two or three times so everyone would understand.

After the show, I had this tremendous sense of relief. I don't know why, but I felt like the weight of the world had been lifted from my shoulders. This show aired on a Tuesday.

On Friday, I got a call and this very frail little voice said, "Hello, Mrs. Jackson. You don't know me. I've only lived in Austin for about six months. I'm a very shy person and I don't have any friends yet to speak of. You're my only friend. I sit down and watch you every day while I eat my lunch.

"But I just had to share something with you. Wednesday of this week, my next-door neighbor had to go to the doctor, and she called and asked me if I could watch her little girl while she was gone. [I think the child was about four years old.]

"She brought the child over, but her mother stayed longer than anticipated and the little girl got hungry. So I gave her some grapes, and she choked on one. Normally, I'm not very self-confident and would have run screaming out of the house, but I remembered the show you did Tuesday on the Heimlich choking method.

"It was like an instant replay. I could see those men in my mind doing that demonstration, and I could see you doing it. I thought, 'Carolyn had never done that before. If she could do it, so can I.' I grabbed that child up and applied the method to her and the grape came up. Mrs. Jackson, I saved that little girl's life because of you. I just had to call and thank you."

By then I was in a cold sweat. Sitting at my desk, I trembled all over while tears streamed down my face.

"Don't thank me, thank the Lord," I told her.

No one can ever convince me that was a coincidence. That was a God incident.

CHAPTER 9
HOCUS POCUS

Each day holds its own special magic.
—SCHOOL POSTER

Television led me into the world of the weird, too. Some of my guests created experiences for me that no other word defines.

One day I interviewed Uri Geller, the famous psychic who can bend objects with his mind. You don't believe he can do it? Well, he made a believer out of me.

The day of my interview with Uri, I had a watch with me that belonged to my daughter Cindi. It wasn't working properly, so I planned to take it to the jeweler to be cleaned and repaired. It was a very pretty watch that I had bought for her in the Virgin Islands. It was designed like a bracelet and had a little top that you opened to see the watch's face. I had the broken watch on one wrist and my own watch on my other wrist.

"Do you always wear two watches?" Uri inquired.

"No, after the show I'm taking this one to be repaired," I replied.

"Maybe I can fix it. Let me see it." He held it, and then handed it back, saying, "No, I can't."

The show went on and Uri bent a few things, including his key to the city, which was still wrapped up. He said he was going to bend it with his mind before taking it from the box.

75

After closing his eyes for a few seconds, he removed the key from the box and sure enough, it was bent!

After the show, Uri said, "I'm sorry I couldn't fix your daughter's watch. Would you like me to try again?"

"Certainly, if you'd like."

"Just put it in your hand and close your palm. Do you feel anything? No? You don't feel anything?"

"No, just the warmth of your hand on mine."

"Well, I'm really sorry I couldn't fix this."

"That's perfectly all right. I'll just take it on to the jeweler's."

I opened my hand and looked at the watch. I was holding it so I could see the top. As I watched, the top that covered the watch face just opened up and bent, right before my eyes.

"Oh, stop it, stop it," I exclaimed, as the cameramen gawked in awe.

"I'm sorry, but I can't," he said.

After the show, when I arrived at the jeweler's, I handed him the watch.

"Could you fix this, please?"

"Hmm, so it got bent?"

"That, and it's not running properly. Maybe it needs cleaning, too."

Opening the watch, the jeweler exclaimed, "Lady, this watch is totally destroyed. The entire mechanism is ruined. What did you do to it?"

"Have you ever hear of Uri Geller? No? Well, he bent it with his mind."

"Sure, lady, sure. Maybe you'd just better take your watch somewhere else."

I decided I'd better get out of there before he had me locked up!

When I told Cindi, I thought she'd be crushed, but instead she was thrilled.

"Mom, who else has a watch that Uri Geller not only bent but totally melted the mechanism? It's probably worth a lot more now than it was before," she exclaimed.

One year, I had several requests to have a guest psychic on the show to make predictions about the New Year. I invited Bertie Catchings, and her appearance became an annual tradition.

The first year, she talked generally about what she expected to happen in the nation and the world. Then she got around to me.

After some general predictions, she said, "I see water. I see a lot of water. I see you on a boat. Are you going on a cruise?"

"No," I said. "Not that I know of. I've never been on a cruise."

Several months later, Cactus walked into my office.

"How would you like to go on a cruise?" he asked.

"You're kidding."

"No, I'm not kidding. We're going to do this really big promotional thing and thought you'd be the ideal person to participate.

"The Department of Agriculture is going to sponsor a Texas at Sea program and get lots of people to go on a cruise. They're also going to sponsor a contest where viewers send in recipes using all Texas products. The winner will go on a Caribbean cruise with you. I think it's a marvelous idea."

After Cactus left, it dawned on me that Bertie had told me I'd go on a cruise, and now I was.

I also recalled, however, that Bertie had looked kind of funny and said, "Be careful, don't miss the boat." Now, what the heck had she meant by that?

A UT professor's wife won the recipe contest and wanted her husband to join us on the cruise, so the arrangements were made for the three of us to go. The travel agent cut our schedule a little bit close, so we barely had time to make our plane connections in Dallas. Worse still, we would have only about an hour to make the ship after we arrived in Miami.

Arriving in Dallas, we discovered our connecting plane had been delayed in the East, so we had to change airlines. We had flown in on Braniff and had to switch to Continental. I began to worry about my luggage, hoping it made the switch OK on such short notice.

When we arrived in Miami, sure enough, my luggage was nowhere to be found. The couple's was there, but mine was not, and we had about thirty minutes to get to the ship.

I called the ship's public relations representative, who was to escort us. He said, "Come on, don't worry about your luggage."

"Joe, I can't go on a week's cruise with only the clothes I have on."

"Don't worry, come on. We'll buy you some new clothes. Ships don't wait for anybody," he said.

I wasn't satisfied, so I galloped back to Braniff, who acted like they'd never heard of me. I ran to Continental, and they were no better.

So I did what any red-blooded American girl would do when everything went wrong. I started to cry. A skycap spotted my tears.

"Is anything wrong, lady?"

"Yes, everything," I bawled. "They've lost my luggage."

"Have you checked Lost and Found?"

"No, why would it be there?"

"Sometimes it happens." So I ran down there and voilà, there was my luggage.

By then, though, we only had about twenty minutes to get to the ship, and it was about fifteen miles away. We grabbed our luggage, hailed the first cab we saw, and told the cabby, "You've got to get us to the ship and you've got to go fast, because we only have about twenty minutes."

"Lady, sit back and relax. It's OK," the cabby soothed me. With that, he took off, got about five miles down the expressway, and ran out of gas!

Apparently this scenario wasn't new to this jerk, because he had a gas can. "Don't worry," he said, rushing off to a nearby gas station. He filled up the tank, and we took off again.

By then, we had ten minutes to go ten miles. "There's no way we're going to make this," I moaned to myself. That cabby drove so fast. I honestly believe he went faster than the plane we flew in on.

We reached the pier, and I could hear the ship blowing its horn. Apparently, Joe, the PR guy, had alerted them we would be running late, because as the cab pulled in, three guys ran out, grabbed our luggage, and ran with it.

Another man picked me up and practically threw me onto the ship just as the gangplank was going up—just like you see in the movies but doubt ever really happens.

When I landed on my feet on the deck, everyone lining the railings applauded, yelling, "They made it, they made it!"

How many times I have thought back to the day when Bertie Catchings said to me, "Water. Boat. You're going on a cruise, but don't miss the boat."

* * *

And, then there was "The Phantom"—one of the mysteries that happened at KTBC that has not been solved to this day. I hope if The Phantom reads this book, he or she will come forward.

Over the course of about a year, I began to receive little notes, always signed "The Phantom." Sometimes there was also a little gift, maybe a flower or a candy bar. I never knew what to expect. They came at real crazy times, no special time of the year. They all had a little face drawn on them, which I assume was the face of The Phantom.

The first time I got one, it was typed: "I love you, Mrs. Jackson. The Phantom." That's all there was to it. I didn't think much of it. I thought it was just someone cutting up and having fun and I'd find out who it was. I soon forgot about it.

Several months later, there was another note. And then others. Sometimes it would be on my desk. Sometimes it was waiting for me in the studio. One time I even found a note in my car. It was really weird. I approached everybody in the station, asking them if they were The Phantom. They all looked at me like I was crazy.

One day I got one that said, "Roses are red and white and yellow. Please let me be your fellow. The Phantom." Many months passed and there was another one. This time it was just a drawing of The Phantom with stars in his eyes. It looked like his ears were shaking, with little hearts all around, and in great big letters it said, "SMACK, The Phantom." More months, then another note.

"My heart is broke, I sadly sigh, you never look me in the eye. The Phantom strikes again."

Months later, another note. "I'm back, I'm back, don't get off track. 'Cause, remember, ducks go quack. The Phantom."

The next one I loved. "My love is too strong, there's no other way. I'll be in your stocking come Christmas Day. The Phantom strikes again." A gift came with it.

Right after Christmas, another. The Phantom looked very disgruntled. His eyes were crossed, and he almost looked like he had horns coming out of his head.

The note read, "I'm mad as hell. I'm very miffed. Christmas is over and I didn't get a gift. The Phantom."

That was the last I ever heard from The Phantom. To this day, I don't know who it was.

Please, Phantom, ease my mind!

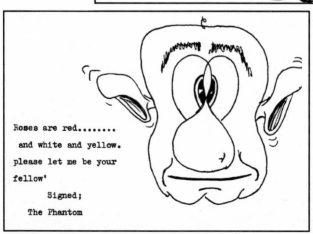

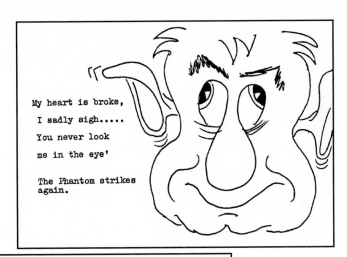

My heart is broke,
I sadly sigh.....
You never look
me in the eye'

The Phantom strikes
again.

My love it too strong,
There's no other way.
I'll be in your
stocking come
Christmas day'

The PHANTOM
strikes again.

I'm mad as hell......
I'm very miffed.
Christmas is over
...and I didn't
get a gift'

THE PHANTOM

CHAPTER 10

WHY ME?

Evil often triumphs, but never conquers.
—CHURCH BULLETIN

If my television career had any adverse effects on my family, I was never aware of it. No celebrity status at home—I was just wife and Mom. They were my balance, my anchor.

I'm sure at times it must have frustrated Chily for me always to be in the spotlight and he in the background, but apparently he never felt threatened, because he handled each situation with grace and style.

One night at a Country Dinner Playhouse cocktail party, a woman walked up to him and said, "How does it feel to be Mr. Carolyn Jackson?"

He smiled and shot back, "It feels great—I taught her everything she knows."

Another day, several teenage girls were at our house, talking and giggling in the den. I couldn't help overhearing their conversation as they oohed and aahed at daughter Carol about my being on TV.

One said, "It must be just awesome having your mom on television."

Quick-witted Carol replied, "Yeah, it's great. I can tune her out anytime I want to." I learned that God is there for you when life pierces your heart in the most painful manner.

Chily proudly shows off his TV wife.

Carolyn with her supportive family, Chily, Carol, and Cindi.

One thing I was not prepared for as a television personality was the fact that you are a prime target for gossip. I've never been able to figure out why anyone would derive any joy from starting malicious rumors or participating in character assassination, but apparently there are those who get their kicks doing this. I have suffered my share of slings and arrows.

One of my daughters once told me, "You know, Mom, you're very vulnerable because everyone knows you. It wouldn't be any fun to talk about Jane Doe or Mary Smith, because nobody knows them."

I suppose she's right, because I look at people who enjoy national acclaim and imagine the horror they must feel when they see their names dragged through the mud in the tabloids and know the stories aren't true.

Someone started a vicious rumor that Chily and I were separated and were getting a divorce. Apparently, it was rampant before I ever even heard about it.

But one day a dear friend had the courage to call me and say directly, "I just want to ask you something. Perhaps it's none of my business, but I want to set the record straight."

"Sure, what is it?"

"Well, I was at a church meeting this morning and you were the topic of conversation. Everyone there had heard you and your husband were separated and maybe he was having an affair, maybe you were having an affair. Are you and Chily having any trouble?"

I was so taken aback, I just listened to her in shocked disbelief.

"Of course we're not having any trouble. How on earth could something like that get started?"

"I don't know, but when I go to the next meeting, I'll see to it they all know the truth."

I told her how much I appreciated that. When I went home, I told Chily and we kind of laughed about it and didn't give it too much thought, but as the weeks and months rolled on, the talk got worse and worse.

As rumors finally trickled back to my ears, I was supposed to be dating some Country-Western guy. I don't know who Chily was supposed to be having an affair with, but the ugly tale just seemed to go on and on and on.

I did everything I could to try to trace it down, without too much success at that point. Believe me, after awhile it was not funny anymore. It began to really, deeply hurt. I didn't want my family to be affected by this, but there's not much you can do about it.

Even Don Blavier, the newsman who did the news on my show and who was an Episcopal minister, came up to me one day laughing and said, "Guess what I heard at church."

"What?"

"That you and your husband are separated and you and I are an item."

Get this—he was an Episcopal minister, married with three children. I think it's ironic that a lot of these rumors were floating around churches, of all places. It was almost unbelievable.

Finally, someone called a friend of mine in Taylor and said, "We understand your friend is getting a divorce."

"What friend?"

"Carolyn Jackson."

She just died laughing and said, "Well, that couldn't come at a funnier time, because they are in Hawaii at this very moment, celebrating their twenty-fifth wedding anniversary and having a blast."

Chily and Carolyn celebrate their anniversary.

But everywhere we went, I felt eyes were staring at me and people were questioning my character. I cannot tell you the extent of pain you endure when you're the victim of something evil that you can't seem to do anything about.

Chily and I continued to go everywhere together. We were seen constantly in each other's company. Every time our family went out together, we acted like a happy family, because that was what we were.

This malicious gossip continued for over a year. Finally, many friends began to come to me and say they'd set the record straight wherever they could.

Once something like this has happened to you, even though it is obvious that it is not true, there's always a certain element of the public that believes it. They seem to want to believe it—I don't know why. Maybe they think it makes us more human if we've gone through that sort of suffering.

I have tried many times to examine this and to determine why anyone would have wanted to start such a rumor. Over about two years, after much investigative work, I finally narrowed it down to the person I think started the whole ugly saga.

I don't intend to name her here, but if she reads this book, she'll know who she is and she'll know the great pain she caused me during this terrible time, this heart-wrenching trauma. I just hope and pray she never has to go through anything like it, that no one ever starts such a vicious rumor about her.

During this torment, I even received some mail, fortunately not a great deal, where the writer would say things like, "I've always admired you so and always thought you were such a good role model. Why are you destroying your life and your image by having marital problems?" Of course, these people didn't sign the letters. You have no way of retaliating.

I don't know how I could have stood it without my family's loving support. Usually such mail would arrive at the station, and sometimes it was terribly hard to go on the air. I'd go home and cry and cry and cry, and the family was always there for me.

The girls would say, "Mom, it's OK. We know it's not true, you know it's not true, Dad knows it's not true, so you've just got to put all this out of your mind." But that didn't keep it from hurting.

Finally, one day Chily said, "You've got to get hold of yourself and not let this bother you anymore. Just put it all in God's hands and let Him be in charge of this. You just put it out of your mind, because there's not anything you can do about it." He was so right.

Finally, the tale died down, but about a year later it cropped up again. This time it didn't last quite as long. One of the beauties of this book will be to let people know that it indeed was not true, but that I suffered terribly through the whole ordeal.

Despite the rumors, Chily and I have celebrated our fiftieth wedding anniversary.

The gossip problem was rather implausible, because I recognized and accepted my responsibility as a person in the limelight. I tried at all times to live up to that responsibility. I always conducted myself in a professional manner and tried never to do anything to discredit the station, myself, or my family.

Many people in the public eye, whether they be broadcasters or politicians or movie stars or athletes, don't accept that responsibility. They don't care what other people think. But I did care and worked very diligently at being the kind of person people would want to see on TV and would welcome into their homes.

It's ironic that I tried so hard to be professional, but still became the victim of malicious gossip. I believe God must have thought I badly needed a lesson in patience, forbearance, and loving my enemies.

CHAPTER 11

THE SHOW MUST GO ON

Learn from yesterday, live for today, hope for tomorrow.
—CHRISTIAN PLAQUE

As much as I loved my television job, sometimes going on the air was almost impossible.

Television personalities are supposed to go on with the show, no matter what is occurring in their personal lives. I always tried my best to be a real trouper, but it wasn't always easy.

I hosted a gentleman on my show once a month. His name was Edmunds Travis, and he was perhaps the most remarkable man I've ever known.

He was in his seventies and had total recall. He was a newspaperman who, at age twenty-one, became the managing editor of the *San Antonio Light*. Later he was the editor and part owner of the *Austin American-Statesman* from 1916 to 1925. In 1925 Mr. Travis announced he was retiring for life at the age of thirty-five but returned to work for newspapers in Austin and Houston.

In 1940 he turned to a new profession—public relations. He could always be seen at the state capitol. He was as much a fixture there as the pictures of the governors. Everyone knew, liked, and respected him.

What most amazed everyone was his memory. For example, in

the 1920 elections, he could tell you who ran, who won, and, at the inauguration, where the winner's wife sat.

He also possessed total recall about the great literary works. He could quote endlessly from Shakespeare or the Bible or his favorite poets. He was absolutely astounding. From the first day, I thought he was the greatest man I had ever met.

He was on the show with me once a month and would recount events that happened long ago in Austin or Texas. He never used any notes. He would just sit there and talk, and the viewers were spellbound.

Each month after the show, Mr. Travis would take me to either the Headliners or another club for lunch. We'd sit in one of those clubs and talk for another two hours. In the several years we did this, he never told me the same story twice. Most of us are guilty of that, but not Mr. Travis.

Every story was always more fascinating than the one before. Often, at lunch, he'd tell me the little inside stories he couldn't tell on the air. At one point I begged him to write a book.

"Aw, that's too much like work. I don't want to work."

He didn't want to tape record his tales, either. He'd say, "Let's just enjoy ourselves like we are. Let's not worry about books."

He offered to lend me books. He had converted his garage into an extensive library. Three to five thousand books lined the shelves, and he used no card system of any kind. He could walk right to any book, pull it, and give it to me. I'd read it and return it. He'd put it up, then recommend and offer me another one.

Not only was he so awesome in his recall, but this man had a phenomenal grasp on life and living and making the most of every day.

"Don't worry about the past or future, but live for today and enjoy every minute of it," he'd admonish me.

He was on the show with me for approximately five years. We savored our lunches, and I reveled in it all.

One day, I arrived at the studio and Mary Strickland looked at me a little strangely. I asked her if anything was wrong, and she said, "Oh, no, everything's fine."

I did the show, then found Mary waiting in the hall for me. She said, "We need to talk."

"Okay," I replied, looking at her with some wonder.

"I have some bad news for you. I didn't want to tell you before you went on the air, because I was afraid you might not make it. But Mr. Travis died this morning."

I felt like the world had come to an end. It had just never occurred to me that this man could die. He was the epitome of life and seemed so healthy and strong. I couldn't think of him as dead. I told Mary I'd be okay, but I cried all the way home, all afternoon, and most of the night.

I knew I had to honor Mr. Travis with a tribute on the air, so I sat down the next morning and wrote one. I couldn't seem to stop crying. They put my tribute on the TelePrompTer so I could announce his death and then read the tribute. I was afraid I would burst into tears and be unable to stop sobbing. My eyes were already red and swollen.

My newsman that day was Donald Blavier, my dear Episcopalian minister friend. I'd shared with him many things Mr. Travis had told me.

"I have a tribute to Mr. Travis. Please read it for me, Don. I don't think I can get through it without crying."

"I can, and I will," Don replied, "but I don't think I should. The tribute should come from you. The last thing he would want from you today is sadness. Today is your chance to put all the things he's taught you about life to good use. He wants you to be happy and to remember him as he was."

He patted me. "You can do it. The Lord will be with you."

The light came on and I read my tribute without crying.

"Services will be held today at 2 o'clock for our beloved friend, Edmunds Travis. Edmunds Travis, with his unique little black derby, so symbolic of his complete individualism. Edmunds Travis, with his treasured pipe, a knowledgeable, philosophical man, a man of dignity.

"Edmunds Travis, with a tiny rosebud in his lapel, a kind, gentle man with a deep love and appreciation for the delicate things in life. He was a little man in physical stature, but a giant of a man in character, compassion, and wisdom.

"Edmunds Travis, truly a legend in his own time. Although he no longer stands among us, he remains in our hearts always. I am personally thankful to Edmunds Travis, not only for sharing with us information about the history of Austin and Texas, but also for sharing with us his bountiful joy in living.

"I trust Mr. Travis was aware of the tremendous impact he had on my life. I think of him so often and I will always remember the many things he taught me. I love you, Mr. Travis."

* * *

One night about midnight, we got a call from our daughter Cindi, who was attending Southwest Texas University in San Marcos. I could tell something was wrong, because she was talking very fast and acting really hyper.

"Mom, were you asleep?"

"Of course I was asleep. What's wrong?"

"Well, we just all wanted some hamburgers and Tommy and Walter went to get the hamburgers and—"

"Cindi, what is it? None of this is making any sense."

"Well, there was a wreck. There was a terrible wreck and it was Tommy and Walter."

Tommy was the son of my best friend, and he was also the roommate of Mike, the young man Cindi dated and eventually married. Mike and Tommy were lifelong friends.

"Cindi, how is he?"

"Mom, they've taken him to Brackenridge Hospital. Where are his parents?"

"They're in New Mexico."

"We're at the police station and the police can't locate his parents. I told them if they'd just let me call you, you could find them."

"Cindi, just try to calm down and put one of the policemen on the telephone."

She did, and I explained to him I'd try to find out where Tommy's parents were and get back to them.

He said, "Mrs. Jackson, do not call these people. The information must come from us."

I told him I understood, and Cindi got back on the phone.

I said, "Cindi, how bad is it?"

"Mom, Walter is dead."

"What about Tommy?"

"Mom, get to him fast. He's not going to make it."

"I will, Cindi, I will."

I woke Chily and called a relative of Tommy's and asked them to try to find Tommy's parents and then to call the police, that we were going to the hospital to try to be with Tommy.

We dressed and drove ninety miles per hour to Austin. By then, I guess it was 1:30 A.M., and when we got to the hospital, it was too late. Tommy was already dead.

We stayed at the hospital until a member of his family could get there. We were there all night. We got back home about 6:00 A.M., and I knew it would be disastrous to try to go back to sleep. I took a shower, got dressed, and went on over to the station, absolutely devastated.

All the staff was hard hit by the flu and there was no one to replace me. I had to do the show, no matter what.

I talked to Dotti Norwood, my dear friend at KTBC, and she was a great comfort. She told me I'd be okay. I was okay until about 11:00 A.M., when I had a real sinking spell.

"I just don't believe I can do this, Lord," I groaned within my soul.

Going outside to get some fresh air, I took a short walk, and there across the street was St. Mary's Catholic Church.

I thought, "I'll just go over there." I'm not a Catholic, but I felt such solace there and felt the presence of the Lord. I bowed my head, and said, "Lord, you know I'm physically exhausted and emotionally drained. But there are people over there counting on me today. Even though I know You're always with me, please let me feel Your presence a little closer today."

I thanked Him, left the church, and went back over to the studio.

It was about 11:30 A.M. when I walked back in, and that's the last thing I remember until 12:30 P.M. I don't remember who my guest was that day, or what either of us said. It is totally blocked out.

The first thing I remember is that the show was over. I left the set and asked Dana, who was walking from the control room, "What time is it?"

"It's 12:30."

"That means the show's over."

"Yes, it's 12:30, it's always over at 12:30," he replied, giving me a puzzled look.

Dotti was waiting in the hall as I came from the studio. She put her arms around me and said, "You were just great. No one would have ever known. How did you do it?"

I said, "Dotti, *I* didn't." She seemed to understand.

* * *

Television personalities sometimes fail to realize what a tremendous impact we have on our viewers and the grave responsibility we occasionally must show them.

I still shiver over an incident that has bothered me for many years. One day, a call came to the switchboard. Mary Strickland was covering and talked to a very distraught woman.

The caller said, "I have to talk to Carolyn Jackson right now."

Mary, always very poised, said, "Ma'am, I'm sorry, but she's on the air right now, and I can't put you through to her."

"But you have to, you have to!"

"Well, she can't possibly talk to you until she gets off the air, but if you'll give me your name and number, I'll have her call you just the moment she's finished."

"You don't understand, I'm about to commit suicide. I have to talk to her."

"Ma'am, Carolyn would not want you to do that. She loves you very much and she wants to talk to you. If you'll just tell me where you are and give me your number, I'll have her call you the minute she walks out of the studio."

"She can't. I'm in a phone booth. She can't call me."

"Yes, she can. Just give me the number there at the phone booth, and she will call you. Meanwhile, you might want to call this number," Mary said, giving her the suicide hotline number.

"No, no, I will call Carolyn back. What time does she get off?"

"She gets off at 12:30. I'll send someone up there to grab her the minute she gets off and she will call you." They sent someone and they explained the situation. I went numb all over. I shuddered to think a total stranger out there somewhere was hurting so much and wanted to talk to me.

I went downstairs and I waited, and waited, and waited. And the call didn't come. Someone finally brought me some lunch, as I was afraid to leave the phone. I waited until 4:00 P.M., but the call never came.

I finally had to finish up my work and go home. It was so devastating. I don't know to this day what happened to that woman. I don't know whether she carried out her threat, or whether she called that hotline and they helped her. It certainly brought home to me what a tremendous responsibility we in the media have and how close some of our viewers feel to us.

CHAPTER 12
LYNDON, LADY BIRD, AND ME

Happiness is found along the way—not at the end of the road.
—UNKNOWN

Working for a radio and television station owned by a president and first lady of the United States is a unique experience.

Lyndon and Lady Bird Johnson had a penthouse on the fifth floor of our building. When business or social activities brought them to Austin, that's where they stayed. The staff's clue they were in residence was the big limo in the garage—plus the presence of the Secret Service men in the lobby.

I'd never known any Secret Service men before, but I quickly gained great respect for them, their understanding families, and their profession. They each had an outgoing personality and a fabulous sense of humor, and they performed their duties in a professional manner.

I always looked forward to the days when agents Jim Hardin and Mike Howard were there. They could turn a drab day into a sunny one with their quick wit and special brand of teasing.

One day, a few station employees had a chance to watch the Secret Service men in action. A new girl at the station never had seen President Johnson in person. When she stepped into the elevator on the third floor, she realized there were several Secret

Service men inside, standing in front of a very tall man. It occurred to her it probably was President Johnson standing behind them.

Desperately wanting a glimpse of him, she turned her head back to look as the elevator door opened on the first floor. At exactly that moment, someone opened the door of the adjacent newsroom and, not watching where she was going, she bumped into it.

Startled, she let out a scream and the action began! Unaware of the reason for her scream, the Secret Service men grabbed the president, threw him to the floor, and covered him. Fortunately, there was no cause for alarm, but to observe the Secret Service men reacting so quickly and effectively was quite a sight.

The Johnsons seldom participated in the day-to-day operation of the station. That duty was left in the capable hands of Mr. Kellam, the station's general manager. However, one day word trickled down to me that they'd be extremely pleased if I would interview Harry Middleton, director of the LBJ Library. I quickly obliged.

After the interview, I went to the lobby to check my messages. Spotting news director Joe Roddy and Mike Howard outside, I went out to say hello and get some fresh air.

"Hey, kid, I have a compliment for you," Mike said.

"Good—what is it?"

"The Big Man was watching your interview, and after it was over, he said, 'I like that girl—she's good.'"

"What are you talking about?"

"The man upstairs."

"God?"

"No—the Big Man in the penthouse!"

"President Johnson?"

"Yes."

"'That girl'—you mean to tell me I work for this man and he doesn't even know my name?"

With that, Joe Roddy put in his two cents' worth.

"Just be grateful he didn't say 'I *don't* like that girl. Get rid of her.'"

"You just wait, Joe. I'm going to be so good, the next time he sees me, he'll know my name!" The next time came at the annual Christmas party.

I was seated at a table with Chily, Joe Roddy and his wife,

Nancy, and Jay Hodgson and his wife, Barbara. The big moment arrived when the Johnsons and their entourage entered the ballroom.

President Johnson walked directly to our table and extended his hand to me.

"Good evening, Carolyn." He then proceeded around the table and the room, greeting everyone.

I dug my elbow into Joe's ribs and snippily remarked in a sing-song voice, "Nanee, nanee, boo boo—he knows my name!"

Snorted Joe, "Nanee, nanee, boo boo—you have on a name tag as big as your head. After all, the man can read!"

Every woman needs a Joe Roddy in her life to keep things in perspective.

I had been forewarned that President Johnson would dance with every lady at the party. I had lamented that fact as Chily and I dressed for the occasion.

"What do you say to a president when you dance with him?"

"I can't believe you'd ever be at a loss for words!"

But when my turn came for a twirl around the dance floor with the Big Man, I knew my worries had been for naught, for indeed he was a big man.

I was in flats and he in cowboy boots, which meant my eye level was somewhere just about his belt buckle. To have looked up and tried to carry on a conversation would have put a crick in my neck.

So rather than talk, I settled for quietly trying to show him I was probably the best dancer he'd ever had the pleasure of waltzing around the floor.

Lots of redecorating was going on at the station, and Lady Bird was personally overseeing the decorating of my office.

She came in to chat with me one day about my choice of colors, styles, etc. She put me so at ease that I soon forgot I was talking to the first lady and felt I was exchanging ideas with a dear friend.

During her visit, I had a call from Chily to discuss our plans for the evening—our daughter Cindi's graduation night. She could tell from my end of the conversation that something important was happening at home.

After I explained the situation to her, she said, "Forget all this. We'll talk about it later. Go home and be with your family."

One day at home, while I was deeply involved in letter writing, the phone rang. A voice said, "Mrs. Jackson, this is the White House. Can you please hold for a call?"

Stunned, and thinking it was a joke, I said, "The what, and hold for whom?"

"The White House. Can you please hold for Mrs. Johnson?" the polite voice said.

"Of course," I stammered.

Mrs. Johnson was calling to ask me to check out some desks in Austin and decide which one I'd prefer.

One day she called me from the ranch about another decorating matter.

Unfortunately, daughter Carol answered the phone. "Hello—the Jackson residence."

"Yes—this is the ranch calling for Carolyn Jackson."

"Just a moment, please. Hey, Mom, the ranch is calling."

"What ranch is that?"

"Without covering the phone, my clown daughter shouted, "The chicken ranch."

She referred to the late and infamous house of ill repute in La Grange made famous by the movie *The Best Little Whorehouse in Texas*.

How does one ever survive teenagers?

Regarding the Johnsons, I suppose the greatest topic of conversation among all of us at KTBC was "the eggs." That's right—I said "eggs."

Periodically, the Johnsons would bring fresh eggs from the ranch to sell to the station employees. They were placed in the reception area, and those who wanted to buy some would pay the receptionist.

The eggs were good and the price was right, about thirty-five cents a dozen, so it was a good deal for me. The funny part was the reaction from others when I told them I bought eggs from President and Mrs. Johnson.

Other station employees apparently got the same reaction, because exchanging egg stories was a favorite pastime. At one of our station parties, we spoofed the Emmys. Several of us received awards for various achievements—strange, comical, unusual, etc.

Our receptionist won the award for the Comment of the Year—"You want me to sell *what?*"

After the Johnsons sold the station, everything changed. We no longer were one big happy family. Instead we became numbers in a large corporation.

I cherish those memories of the unique Johnson days. I'm especially grateful for the opportunity I had to know Lady Bird, who always was gracious to me.

After President Johnson left the White House and returned to Texas, he brought several key staff members with him—among them Tom Johnson (no relation). Tom was a friendly, likable person and one who obviously had a great deal of potential in the broadcasting field.

He quickly and effectively settled into the operation of the TV station. I liked Tom from the beginning and always enjoyed exchanging ideas with him. Recollections of working with Tom bring to mind two favorite stories.

He walked into my office one day and said, "You have the most extraordinary cumes I've ever seen." I didn't have a clue what cumes were, but could tell by the tone of his voice and his grin that this was a compliment.

"Thanks—what are cumes?"

Laughing heartily, he explained that cumes meant that I had a very loyal audience that was growing more loyal every week. After hearing his technical explanation from the ratings book, I decided not to worry about cumes, but to continue concentrating on producing the most interesting show possible every time I went on the air.

The day before I was to leave on a cruise representing the station, Tom appeared in my office.

"Isn't St. Thomas on your itinerary?"

"Yes. Why?"

"Well, I'd like you to say hello to a friend of mine there." He explained that the man was a longtime friend of his and President Johnson's who had been in Washington with them.

St. Thomas is one of my favorite places in all the world to shop, and the last thing I wanted to do was take valuable shopping time to visit someone else's friend. But Tom had always been so nice to me, and I knew he wouldn't ask if it weren't important to him. How could I refuse?

"Sure, I'll be glad to—who is it and how do I find him?"

He wrote down all the information. The gentleman's office was in the midst of the shopping area, which somewhat relieved my fears of not having enough time to find the things on my list.

The gentleman was charming, and we had a delightful visit. To my surprise, he said, "I'm sure you're anxious to shop during your short stay here, so I won't delay you any longer. Where are you planning to shop?"

I told him the name of the store and he said, "Good—I think you'll find everything you want there."

We said our farewells and, with a courtly bow and a kiss on my hand, he sent me on my way.

The most important purchase was to be a watch for Chily. With the aid of a very knowledgeable and polite salesman, I decided on a handsome Omega. It was a bit more than I had planned to spend, but I wanted him to have a good one—one that would last.

The store had an excellent reputation, so I had no qualms about the quality of the watch. After selecting two less expensive, but very lovely, feminine watches for Cindi and Carol, I quickly picked up a few souvenir-type items for co-workers and friends, then headed for the cash register.

As I placed the items on the counter, the sweet young lady smiled and asked my name. That seemed odd, but I brushed it off by assuming it was store policy to call customers by name.

"I'm Carolyn Jackson."

"Mrs. Jackson—welcome. We've been waiting for you. My instructions are to give you a fifty-percent discount on anything you purchase in the store."

"What? Whose instructions?"

When she called his name—guess who? Tom's friend. He owned the store! I couldn't believe my ears.

After returning to the station, I related the whole story to Tom—even the bit about resenting the fact that I had to spend valuable shopping time with his friend—and how it had all turned out to my advantage.

Teasingly, Tom said, "I guess rightfully that Omega watch should be mine."

"You'll have to get it over Chily's dead body. He loves it." To this day, Chily still wears and cherishes that watch.

None of us who worked with Tom Johnson at KTBC have been

Tom Johnson briefs Carolyn and viewers about CBS programming.

surprised at his step-by-step advancement up the career ladder. He's now president of CNN.

* * *

It was one of the coldest days I can ever recall in Texas. One would have thought we were in some remote, frigid region of the world, rather than in the Hill Country.

The occasion—the graveside service for President Johnson at the LBJ Ranch. Any of the KTBC employees and spouses who wished to attend were provided bus transportation from the station to the ranch. The usual jovial group was silent and somber on that dreary winter day. The miles seemed endless.

Although I was adequately dressed for the weather—heavy coat, hat, gloves, scarf, boots—the walk from the bus to the graveside was almost unbearable. Being extremely cold-natured, I wondered if I could make it through the service, for I was already shivering from head to toe. We all huddled together in a vain attempt to warm one another.

The service was moving, but the moment that will forever be etched in my mind is when longtime Johnson family friend and entertainer Anita Bryant stepped forward to sing. The biting, icy wind was piercing my lungs, making breathing difficult and talking almost impossible.

I remember thinking, "How can she possibly do this? How could anyone sing in this weather?"

But she held us all spellbound and teary-eyed with her a cappella rendition of "The Battle Hymn of the Republic." I had never heard it sung more beautifully. Suddenly, a warmth filled my entire body.

Lyndon Baines Johnson was gone, but the legacy he left through his radio and television station would extend his influence for many years to come.

CHAPTER 13
UNDERCURRENTS

Your choices reflect your character.
—SCHOOL POSTER

As the years rolled by, I enjoyed my career more with each passing day. Though often stressful, my job was challenging, exciting, and fulfilling. Going to work each day was a joy. Many people feel trapped in unsatisfying, boring jobs and can't or won't do anything to change it. Those who truly love their work are fortunate, and I was among them.

Little did I know my life was about to undergo some dramatic changes.

During my commute to work one day, I suddenly felt a rush of unexplained uneasiness and sensed something was wrong. I tried to brush my feelings aside, but when I arrived at the station, tension hung ominously in the air. I knew my hunch had been on target—something was terribly wrong.

Finally, someone dropped the bomb—the station had been sold! Rumors ran amok, and for days we all went through the motions of performing our duties with little or no enthusiasm. The unknown is such a fearsome monster. After what seemed like an eternity, we were called together, a proper announcement was made, and the details of the transaction were explained.

Carolyn jokes with the crew before going on the air.

The Los Angeles Times-Mirror had purchased the television station, but the Johnsons had kept the AM-FM radio station. The TV station would keep the call letters KTBC, while the radio station would change to KLBJ. The staff was given the choice of staying with TV or going to radio.

Since television had been my mainstay and my radio limited to occasional reports and commercials, I chose to stay with TV. I must admit, I had some trepidation about my future under new management. I especially hated to see Mr. Kellam leave to become the general manager of the radio station.

Finally, the bigwigs arrived from Los Angeles to greet us and welcome us to the new company. They assured us nothing would change—famous last words! Big corporations always say that. Then you wake up one morning and discover everything has changed.

The new owners brought in a new general manager. Gradually, he met with each of us to define our positions. When my turn came, he assured me he was completely pleased with my program and my performance.

He suggested changing the name of the show from *Woman's*

World to *The Carolyn Jackson Show,* pointing out that research showed the program was no longer just a women's show, but one that appealed to both sexes and all ages. The name change was fine with me.

He also said he would like me to have a new set—an enlarged and more modern one. He asked if I had any suggestions or recommendations for my show.

"Yes," I told him. "I'd like to have some women on the crew, specifically Mary Strickland as my floor manager."

He assured me this would be done and concluded our conversation saying, "You're doing an excellent job. Continue doing everything just the way you are doing it. Keep up the good work. We're fortunate to have you."

I left his office believing all my worries had been unwarranted. "This is going to turn out okay after all," I told myself.

At first the transition went smoother than I expected. It wasn't until about three months later that I began to notice some disenchantment among the employees, especially the floor crew. They complained about the new manager's sarcastic remarks and his arrogance. My own first confrontation with him was soon to come.

I had a call from one of the major movie companies inviting me on a movie junket. These junkets usually lasted only two days, and when possible they scheduled them on weekends so we didn't have to miss work. Occasionally, they were held during the week. In that event, I would leave immediately after my show for the junket destination, usually New York, Los Angeles, or Dallas. The first evening, the media people had dinner together and then previewed the movie. The next day, we interviewed the stars and then flew home.

The movie companies paid all our expenses and even provided the tapes for the interviews. Our stations were out nothing. Several newspaper critics from the Austin market always were invited, but I felt privileged to be the only TV personality in the area to be included.

In the past I either had taped my show in advance or Cactus Pryor or Jay Hodgson sat in as host for me on the day I was gone. Since the general manager had told me to continue doing everything as I had been doing, I assumed this junket would be no exception. I went into his office to inform him of the date of the junket. I asked if he preferred I pretape a show in advance or have Cactus sit in for me.

Carolyn reflects on interesting guests after her show.

"Why do you want to go on a movie junket?" he asked.

"To interview the stars," I replied, thinking the answer was obvious.

"Nobody wants to watch you interview somebody off in another city."

"Sir, it's not where I interview, but who I interview. My celebrity interviews are always the show's most popular segments. The viewers love them."

"Well, why can't you just interview them here in Austin?"

"Unfortunately, they don't come to Austin. I have to go to them. And it won't cost the station a cent."

"Well, if it's that big a deal to you, then do it. But every time you go, you make sure you tape a show in advance, plus you will have to take a day of vacation when you miss a day here."

I was dumbfounded. But from that day on, I had to use five or six vacation days each year on movie junkets. I wasn't happy with the idea of working on my vacation time, but my only other option was giving up my highly prized interviews. I chose to do the interviews because they were a contributing factor to my high ratings.

My next clash with the general manager was over my intern

program. I had an arrangement with the University of Texas to let one communications student per semester intern with me. The student was required to spend a certain number of hours observing me and performing any duties at the station I believed appropriate to gaining experience.

At the end of the semester, I wrote an evaluation of the student's performance and recommended a grade. The student, in turn, received three hours of college credit.

My daughter Carol was a speech/journalism major at Southwest Texas State University in San Marcos. She asked to do a summer internship with me. I spoke with her professor, who was very much in favor of her doing it. He saw no problem with our mother-daughter relationship.

Because she rode to work with me each day, she spent more hours than were required of her, and I kept her busy. After a couple of weeks, I walked into my office one day and found a very sarcastic memo from the manager on my desk. It read:

"I wondered who that kid was who's been following you around. I asked someone and he said it was your daughter doing an internship. Who authorized you to have an intern? I must have a full explanation and documentation on this for the FCC."

Stunned, I recalled his initial instructions to me to "continue doing everything just the way you are doing it." But once again, I was called upon to defend my actions.

This time I had to justify helping future broadcasters by conducting an intern program. This was my reply:

Memo to: General Manager
From: Carolyn Jackson
RE: Internships

Several years ago, a professor in the Radio-Television-Film Department at UT contacted me about the possibility of allowing a student to do an internship with me. He was primarily interested in having the student observe (under my supervision) in order to gain a better understanding of commercial TV. Also he suggested that I might delegate small responsibilities if I so desired. The student would be with me only a few hours a week—the equivalent of time which otherwise would have been spent in the classroom. At the end of the semester I was to contact him to let him know what I felt the student had learned and to suggest a grade based on attitude, dependability, and of course, knowledge gained. There was no monetary compensation to the student, only the credit received. Station management said it was fine with them if I had no objections to the extra work. I have done this with students periodically ever since.

Last summer Carol did an internship with the newspaper in San Marcos and this summer asked if she might do one with me (six weeks). Dr. Taylor gave his full approval if I were willing. I was reluctant at first because she is my daughter, but after careful thought decided she should not be penalized for that reason and should be given the same opportunity as other students. We discussed it at length and agreed we could operate on a student-teacher relationship rather than a mother-daughter one, which I believe we did. However, I demanded a bit more of her and fortunately, she met the demand.

Even though this is time-consuming for me, I do hope we can continue the intern program either with SWT or UT or both (Southwestern University might be interested, too). I like helping these students (guess it's the school teacher coming out in me). And, I keep thinking back to my college days and how I'd have given my front teeth just to peep in the window at a station—much less get inside and actually observe people in action. There's a selfish motive too. I learn from these kids. Gives me new insight into their way of thinking and very often they come up with creative ideas and worthwhile suggestions. Helps keep me on my toes to avoid ruts and I find myself trying harder and harder to be more professional because they're watching. I've tried very hard to see that the students do not impose on anyone in the station and that they do not in any way interfere with the operation of the station.

Incidentally, I'm proud of my protégés. One is now a buyer with an ad agency, one has his own program in Oklahoma, one is in broadcasting in Europe (the last I heard). Only one was a drop-out—she became ill at midterm and had to leave school. As for my latest—Carol—only time will tell.

Now that I've given you all this background, I need some guidelines on exactly how I should go about documenting the necessary information. I assume you want information only on those students I've dealt with since our last license renewal. Is there some form I should fill out, or should I just provide a written statement of my contact with Dr. Taylor and what is expected of both the student and myself?

* * *

I never received any response to this memo, so I continued working with interns.

CHAPTER 14

DARE TO CHANGE

*To keep on learning and growing, you must risk failure
all your life.*

—SCHOOL POSTER

Time passed and the morale at the station dipped lower and lower.
Several people quit; many were fired. Salary increases were few and
far between. Our innovative ideas were squelched and the wind
knocked out of our sails with each attempt at creativity. The moti-
vation to strive for excellence dwindled. We all felt defeated—the
fun was gone.

The manager posted a sort of "report card" stating all the things
each of us must do if we expected to continue with the company. I
made an appointment to talk with him about my performance. I reminded him of my consistently high ratings and pointed out that
not only was I performing all the duties expected of me, but I was
going the extra mile by spending nearly every weekend judging contests, making personal appearances, and willingly representing the
station in many other ways.

"None of this has translated into a pay increase, nor have I ever
been compensated for expenses incurred while I've darted around
Central Texas doing PR for the station," I told him.

His reply? "You don't need more money, Carolyn. You have

Chily to take care of you." That frosted the cake! I decided I'd better start thinking about life after television.

One evening, I called Mary Denman, my dear friend and confidante. Mary had hosted a television show like mine for many years in San Antonio, but had resigned about a year earlier to do a radio call-in talk show.

When I explained my miserable situation at KTBC, she exclaimed, "Forget TV. Do what I'm doing here. I've never been happier."

"But there aren't any radio talk shows in Austin."

"Well, the time has come. Start one. Be a trailblazer. If anyone can do it, you can."

The more I mulled her advice, the more I liked the idea. I organized my ideas and approached Mr. Kellam at radio station KLBJ.

"Mr. Kellam, Austin is the only major market in Texas that doesn't have call-in talk shows. The time is right. Let's do it before someone else does. Give it a try. Let me co-host a one-hour call-in talk show with Don Lincoln." Don was KLBJ's program director.

"Well, it sounds like a feasible idea, but do you think you'd get enough calls?"

"There's no doubt in my mind. Just listen to WOAI in San Antonio and you'll see how popular their talk shows are—everyone wants to talk." Mr. Kellam had confidence in me, but he didn't want to make a wrong move. After all, he was accountable to the Johnsons for the success or demise of the station. And Don Lincoln was even more skeptical of the idea than Mr. Kellam.

"I don't think I'm prepared for a talk show. I'm not trained for that," he protested.

"Don, you have a wonderful voice, a good background in broadcasting, a keen perspective on events, and you're knowledgeable. You're ideal for it," I insisted.

After gaining Don's reluctant consent and waiting while Mr. Kellam gave the idea thorough consideration, we got the green light to start preparation. I focused my attention on setting up the talk show at KLBJ, meanwhile merely coasting at KTBC. Then came a strange turn of events.

A friend of mine at the NBC affiliate KTVV, Channel 36 (now KXAN), called and asked me to meet her for lunch. She told me that Al Howard, general manager of Channel 36, had gotten wind of my discontent at KTBC and would like to talk to me.

I said, "Why not. What do I have to lose?"

My friend set up the appointment and Al Howard and I met. He asked me if I had a contract at KTBC, and I told him, "No."

"Would you consider doing your show at our station?"

"I'm listening."

First, he offered me a contract. In all my years at KTBC, I had never had a contract. He also offered me more money, more creative freedom, and permission to go anywhere I wanted for interviews—and not on my vacation time. To boot, there would be extra pay when I represented the station at public events. And they even wanted me to host some promotional trips (the travel bug had bitten me by now). It sounded like heaven.

"Before I make a decision, there's one major consideration."

"What is that?"

"I will come only if my director, Dana Martin, can come with me. We're a team."

"That's no problem. We'd be delighted to have a fine director like Dana on our staff."

Suddenly, I was faced with one of my life's most momentous decisions. Not only was I about to launch a new radio show, but I was being romanced by another television station in the same city.

Jumping stations in Austin was unheard of—an unwritten no-no. No one else had made such a bold move. It was done in all other markets, but thus far—not in Austin. I knew I'd be criticized by many for not being loyal to KTBC. I also knew many would applaud my pioneering spirit in daring to make a change.

There was one more huge factor. KTBC was the number-one station in the market. Channel 36 was number three. I sat down with my family to discuss the pros and cons. They offered lots of input.

"After all, Mom," Carol said, "maybe you can help the number-three station become number one."

Added Cindi, "You're not happy at KTBC anymore, so why not give it a try somewhere else?"

"If you don't do it, you may always regret not taking the risk," Chily pointed out.

They all agreed the final decision had to be mine, but whatever I decided, they'd be supportive. Before I made up my mind, I had to talk with Mr. Kellam. What would he say about my going to

Channel 36? Even though he was no longer associated with KTBC, he still had strong emotional ties there. There was nothing to do but ask him.

"Mr. Kellam, does it matter to you which television station I work for?"

"Why do you ask that?"

"Because I'm considering leaving KTBC. Things aren't the same there since you left. I'm just not happy. Channel 36 has made me a tremendous offer, which I think I'll accept."

"So go for it, my dear. Where you work when you're not here is your business. I'm only concerned with your time spent at KLBJ."

That was all I needed. I called Al Howard and accepted the job. I would start in one month.

The only hurdle left was resigning from Channel 7. I prepared my letter of resignation and personally delivered it to our general manager.

After reading my letter, he was livid. He raged at me, "If money is such a big deal to you, go on."

Looking him in the eye, I said, "This isn't about money. It's about happiness, contentment, and opportunity."

I assured him I'd spend the next two weeks making the transition as smooth as possible and would work closely with my replacement.

"I don't want you to stay here two weeks. I want you out of this building today. And I'll get those bastards at 36," he yelled.

With that, I walked out.

Later I learned that he immediately picked up the phone and called Al Howard.

"What in the hell are you doing, stealing my employee?"

"Did you have a contract with her?"

"No."

"If you'd had a contract, I couldn't have hired her. And, too, I couldn't have wooed her over here if she'd been happy there," Al replied.

"Before you came here, we were able to keep the pay scale down, and now you're ruining everything," he bellowed.

Al hung up.

While I cleaned out my desk, the manager barged into the studio and started tearing down my set with his bare hands. The staff thought he'd gone crazy.

He forbade the staff from forwarding my mail and insisted that all callers be told no one knew what happened to me or where I was. They were instructed to say something like, "Carolyn just walked out on us. We don't know where she is, but Donna Axum, the former Miss America, and Cactus Pryor have graciously agreed to fill her spot." Leaving KTBC behind, Dana and I began making preparations for our debut on Channel 36 in one month.

But my most immediate concern loomed larger—the premiere of my talk show on KLBJ in just three days.

Marquee at the Frank Irwin Center.

CHAPTER 15
STARTING OVER

Today is a good day if I make it that way.
—MY GRANDMOTHER

Radio is my first love. That's where I began my broadcasting career, and its intimacy with the listeners makes it very special. In many ways, radio is more challenging than television, because unlike television, everything on radio must be expressed verbally. In television, a picture is worth a thousand words and you can show events without saying a word. In radio there can be no "dead air." There must be constant talk, and it can't be just idle chatter. It has to be meaningful communication.

Starting a radio talk show, especially in a town where there is none, brings a special set of difficulties, because no one wants to be the first listener to call in. Before our first show, Don and I threatened our families and friends within an inch of their lives if they didn't call in that first day. In the business that's called "planting some calls." We had to get the ball rolling, so I confess we planted a few calls that first show. Once they started coming in, we never had to worry again. Plenty of calls poured in.

From the beginning, Don and I had an extraordinary rapport. We didn't always agree on everything, but we could disagree in a professional manner and always maintain respect for one another.

114

Don Lincoln and Carolyn with actress Rhonda Fleming before an interview at KLBJ.

The show had a magazine format, with guest experts talking about a wide variety of topics. Don and I would throw some questions at the experts, then we would invite the audience to call in.

We had segments on medicine and health, business and finance, cooking, home maintenance, gardening, auto repair, the law, travel, education, and many other topics.

Gardening shows were always popular. Then–county horticulturist Ted Fisher would come and answer questions about when to plant, when to prune, how to fertilize, and other topics.

Sometimes county extension agents would visit to answer questions about cooking, cleaning, and organizing the home.

We had lots of programs on education. People from every level would talk about current projects or problems in the schools and how they could be improved.

When our guest was a medical professional, he or she was always deluged with questions from people concerned about their health.

At tax time, IRS officials came on the air to answer questions from beleaguered taxpayers having trouble filling out their tax forms.

Travel shows were always enthusiastically received. Listeners loved hearing where the best bargains were, the hot spots at the time, tourist traps to avoid, and tips on efficient packing.

Authors were always welcome guests, especially new ones who needed help promoting their first books.

We occasionally had a psychic, which always meant a wild and crazy show. People would call in wanting to know exactly what was in store for them. Although many people don't believe in psychics, others are true believers and thought their predictions were wonderful.

From time to time, we would invite elected officials to be on the show. We would have the mayor, city council members, or county commissioners. If there were certain issues facing the area that were very pertinent, we would try to have these people on a more regular basis at that time so people could talk to them and let them know what the citizens thought and what they wanted.

Occasionally, we took polls. One time the legislature was trying to decide whether to institute daylight saving time. We took a poll and the majority of our callers were against it, but the legislators went right ahead and voted to go on daylight saving time.

Our listeners loved talking to stars who came to town to play in various productions or to do promotions. It was almost like they could sit down personally with the star and visit over a cup of coffee.

One of my best guests was Herb Kelleher, the president of Southwest Airlines. I met him in the coffee shop to visit briefly before we went on the air. He whipped out some little travel glasses that folded up to about the size of a half-dollar.

"Oh, I love those fold-up glasses," I said. "I want some so badly, but I don't know anywhere to get them other than Hong Kong. Since Southwest Airlines doesn't fly there, I guess I don't have a chance of getting over there anytime soon."

Herb just laughed and brushed it off, and nothing more was said. About two weeks later, I received a little package in the mail. When I opened it up, there was a pair of those little glasses, neatly enclosed in a silk case. And there was a note from Herb, telling me he hoped I would enjoy my glasses. The note explained that he couldn't send the complete glasses, since he didn't know my prescription, but at least there were the frames.

"What a truly nice gesture," I thought. I have those glasses to this day and they go on all my trips. Of course, everyone wants to know where I got them, and then they want some. They are so handy for traveling, because they fold up into practically nothing.

Gossip columnist Liz Smith was another great guest on my show. She's a Texas native and had written a book, so she was on the talk show circuit. It gave her a chance to come home and visit her mother, who lives near Bastrop, and talk about her book on the air.

Ken Wallingford had been one of my television guests. He was perhaps the first Austinite to return home who had been a prisoner of war in Vietnam.

I very much wanted to have him on my radio show, too. When I called to invite him, though, he was extremely reluctant. "What are you going to ask?" he wanted to know.

"Ken, I can't give you a list of questions, because I don't know myself. I let my guest guide. I like it to flow just like two friends talking to each other," I replied.

I assured him that if there were anything we should not discuss because of security, certainly I wouldn't approach it. All he would have to say was, "I'm not at liberty to talk about that." I told him approximately what I thought the audience would like to know and said that's generally how the conversation would go, unless he led me in another direction, and he finally agreed to be my guest.

He had one other request. "While I'm there, I would very much like to meet Lady Bird Johnson," he said. I told him I thought that could be arranged, and it was.

You could have heard a pin drop in the studio while he talked. Oddly enough, no calls came in. We kept inviting people to call, and finally someone did. Said the caller, "Carolyn, I think the reason not many have called is because we are so fascinated with what he's saying, we don't want to interrupt him." Ken handled the questions and dealt with the public in a most charming manner.

Former governor Ann Richards was a frequent guest when she was a Travis County commissioner, especially when she was campaigning. Politicians were always happy to be on with us when they were running for office. Ann appeared on the show a number of times and was on the air for a full hour, answering questions. After she became governor, I was disappointed that we lost touch.

One of the funniest experiences I ever had was one day when we had scheduled a priest to come and talk about Austin's celebration for Our Lady of Guadalupe. When airtime came, no priest appeared. So we had an open-line segment, which allowed people to call in and talk about any subject they desired. In the midst of the program, the door opened and the receptionist ushered in two women.

She mouthed "Our Lady of Guadalupe" to me, sat them down at the table, and placed a microphone before each one. One woman was Hispanic and appeared to be in her forties. She was well dressed and seemed very poised and pleasant.

The other woman was elderly and appeared very ill at ease. She was wearing a wig that was slightly askew and she seemed to be generally in disarray. I felt sorry for her, because she looked so uncomfortable.

At the break, off the air, I said to the women, "I need to get some information about you and we'll talk to you in just a few minutes." I turned to the first woman and asked her name. She gave it to me and I asked her title. "I'm the overall coordinator," she replied.

"What phase of this do you want to talk about?"

"I want to talk about all of it."

"OK." Well, I thought, if she's going to talk about all of it, what's this other woman going to talk about? I turned to the second woman and asked her name. She told me, and I wrote it down.

"What is your title?" I asked.

"I don't have any title."

It dawned on me I had two women instead of a priest, so I said, "Where is your priest?"

"I don't know."

"Well, what do you want to talk about?"

"I don't want to talk about anything. I just came here to apply for a job."

Picture this scenario. These two women arrived at the station door at the same time. Our receptionist, thinking that because they arrived at the same time, they were together, and knowing they were late, grabbed them and ushered them up the steps. She seated them and put a microphone in front of them.

Imagine what must have been going through that second woman's mind! She was just applying for a job, and here she was seated before a microphone and I was demanding, "Where's your priest?"

It's a wonder the poor woman didn't faint! I lost complete control. I got so tickled and was in such hysterics, I could not contain myself even after we got back on the air. Don had to take over for a few minutes while I regained my composure.

When it was all over, I told the staff, "We probably owe that poor woman a job for having put her through such an ordeal. It's a wonder we didn't cause her to have a heart attack."

Hosting that talk show for KLBJ was one of the most fun things I've ever done in my life. It was a joy to get up in the morning. Every day was going to be different. Every day I knew I would meet new people via the telephone. Every day was a new and exciting challenge.

After awhile the show was so popular that we extended it from one hour to two hours, and then the station added a classified ads talk show program at noon, which local personality Joyce Isaacs hosted. They also added a sports talk show in the evening, so now we had about four or five hours of talk. Later they decided to have an afternoon talk show, too, so we went to mostly all talk.

Radio is very intimate. Sometimes too intimate, as I learned one day when I answered a call on the air and a female voice said, "Carolyn, you're going to die." I couldn't believe I had heard her correctly.

"What?" I gasped. The woman repeated her frightening statement.

By then, Don had cut her off. We were on a seven-second delay, so when someone said something they shouldn't, we were able to cut it off before it went on the air. However, we had her terrifying words on tape.

When we went to a break, I asked Don, "What did she say? Did she say what I think she did?"

"Yes, she did," he said.

The moment the show was over, we listened to the tape and Mr. Kellam called the police. They came, listened, and said they didn't believe there was a murderer out there, that it sounded more like a kook call.

However, they did suggest I take certain precautions. They said I should get an unlisted phone number and that I should be very careful going to my car from the station, especially if someone knew I was going to be there.

I couldn't get an unlisted number in Taylor, but not everyone knew I lived there. We did maintain an apartment in Austin at the time, so I secured an unlisted number there.

For several months after that, I got some weird calls at my apartment where the unlisted phone would ring and nobody would say anything. It was obvious someone was on the line. They said nothing, but I could hear them breathing. The calls came frequently enough that I knew they weren't just picking my number at random.

The behavior was obviously very calculated. Someone was either trying to get on my nerves or drive me crazy. I never did find out who it was, and fortunately they made no attempt to carry out their threat to kill me.

Meanwhile, my debut at KTVV was exhilarating. The station had run an extensive newspaper campaign announcing my switch. So, most of my viewers figured out where I was even if KTBC wouldn't tell them.

Loyal friends like Neal Spelce, John Bustin, even a couple of the Secret Service men, sent me flowers and cards of encouragement. After the first week, an avalanche of congratulatory letters poured in.

Most of my regular guests from KTBC, such as home economist Janelle Jones, moved with me. KTVV provided Janelle a beautifully equipped kitchen for the cooking segment and my new set was warm and welcoming.

I quickly settled into the routine of broadcasting the radio show from 9:00 to 11:00 A.M. and then dashing over to Channel 36 for my TV show at noon. Often, I could host the same guests on both shows. The audience loved it. They could hear and talk with the guests on the radio, then see them during my TV interview. The two shows complemented and boosted each other.

Al Howard kept all his promises, including travel. The station sponsored a trip to Switzerland and invited viewers to go along, with me as hostess. We had forty-five people sign up.

One of them was my dear friend and neighbor Jo Streit. Seeing Switzerland had been a lifelong dream of hers. She invited her son, Brad, to go along.

Brad was a student at Stephen F. Austin State University, majoring in radio/television/film. He had always shown great interest in my work and occasionally visited me in the studio.

I got the bright idea that perhaps Brad could film the trip. We could share the trip via film with all our viewers upon our return. Everyone liked the idea, including one of Brad's professors, who agreed to give him college credit if he did a good job. The news department provided a camera and gave Brad a crash course in its operation.

The trip was a tremendous success, including Brad's film. We edited it into five ten-minute segments and played one each day the week after our return. Viewers were intrigued. Many said the film and my narration made them feel as though they had been on the trip with us.

About six months later, the station sponsored another trip, a Caribbean cruise. This time, forty-eight viewers went along.

Even though each trip had a crisis or two, I handled the situations to everyone's satisfaction. Along the way, I discovered a couple of things about myself. I liked taking care of people and I liked being a troubleshooter. Travel was becoming more and more fascinating for me.

I was thriving on the challenge of doing both radio and TV. It was stressful, but it was a good kind of stress. I loved every minute of it. After a couple of years of this beloved chaos, I considered myself ever so fortunate. I had the best of worlds—radio, TV, and travel. Life was sweet.

It was the calm before the storm. A bomb was about to drop *again*.

Mr. Kellam died. What a tremendous loss to the industry, the community, and especially to those of us who had worked for him and had such respect and admiration for him.

Pat Nugent, Luci Johnson's husband, took over as general manager of KLBJ.

Pat and I got along well. He was a staunch supporter of the talk show format and wanted to expand it even more. Things were going quite well, but then Luci and Pat had domestic difficulties and were divorced. Suddenly, Pat was out of the picture.

The station brought in a new manager from San Angelo, who was different, to say the least. He was aloof, difficult to approach, and almost impossible to talk to. He gave us no indication about how he felt about the talk format. We couldn't read him at all.

After a few months, word on the street was that KLBJ was

about to chuck the talk show format and go to all music. We kept hearing these rumors, even from people at other stations. We couldn't believe our ears. There had been no indication within the station that a major change was under way. Besides, all our shows were growing in popularity. The ratings were rising, and Austin had truly accepted talk radio. But the rumors persisted.

Finally, Don and I decided to confront the manager about the rumors.

"Oh, yeah, as of May 15 we're not going to do this anymore," he mumbled.

"Shouldn't we have been the first to know?" May 15 was two weeks away.

"I was going to get around to telling you. We've decided to do away with talk and just have music again on KLBJ. So after May 15, we won't need you anymore." That was the end of the first round of talk shows on KLBJ.

The Lord was with me, though, and showed me the good in what I considered to be a devastating event. One of the most rewarding things about it was the great influx of calls and letters from people far and wide telling the station how much they missed Don and me and saying what a disservice it was to the community to take us off the air.

I even received two or three bouquets of flowers. One was from a young man in Austin who said he wanted so much to meet me personally.

"Could I come to meet you? I would be glad to drive to Taylor."

I told him I'd be delighted. He turned out to be a high school senior. He wanted to tell me that he had been a fan from my very first show and he wanted me to know how much he had learned from the radio shows. He said when he couldn't be at home to listen, he would tape them. It was very rewarding.

I guess it's just knowing there were so many people out there that I had touched in some way that made it all so difficult to give up. But it was so rewarding to have done it at all. It was truly a fabulous experience.

I missed radio tremendously, but I was still doing TV at the time, so that filled the void somewhat.

CHAPTER 16

NOT AGAIN!

Giving up is not an option.

—SCHOOL POSTER

As if losing my KLBJ talk show weren't enough, life at Channel 36 took a dramatic downturn. Al Howard resigned as general manager to accept a position with a station out of state.

"I'd love to have you work for me at the new station if you're willing to leave Texas," he said.

Tempting as it was, that was not an option for me. Not only was my family too firmly rooted in Central Texas, but it wasn't practical financially. Chily was the major breadwinner in our family—my salary was merely supplemental.

When the new manager was named, I was swept with déjà vu. Been there, done that! My intuition was right—things gradually began to change, and I felt myself once more on an out-of-control roller coaster.

He canceled my noon show and rescheduled it for 9:00 A.M. He preferred a male host, so my duties were reduced to movie reviews and special reports. The handwriting was on the wall—my days there were numbered.

"Stop letting these people hurt you time after time. Get out of this damn business. You are so talented, so versatile—do something else," Chily pleaded.

I knew he was right—it was time to move on. But I also knew broadcasting was in my blood and being without it would be like losing a best friend.

After admitting to myself that God had slowly closed all the doors and apparently my "on-the-air" days were over, I fervently prayed for guidance:

"Dear Lord, I realize that the desires of my heart and what's best for me are not always the same. I know You have a purpose for my life. Please lead me to that purpose and put me to work. Amen."

While waiting and wondering what direction my life would take next, I received a call from a friend who said a couple of gentlemen from out of town were trying to secure the license for a new TV station in Austin. They wanted to meet with me and enlist my help. Out of curiosity, I met them for lunch.

Steve Beard was a media buyer from Dallas and Darrell Cannon owned a TV station in Wichita Falls. They asked if I'd be interested in serving as a consultant for several months, assisting them with FCC ascertainments and helping them get acquainted with community leaders. They acknowledged that my name recognition and reputation would be a tremendous asset to them in their efforts to obtain the license.

And what would I get out of all this? Of course, they would pay me for the time I spent working with them. And, if they received the license, they wanted me to be involved in the station. They definitely wanted me to produce and host a weekly public affairs program. There was also the possibility of my participating in the overall operation of the station and receiving a small percentage of the profits.

Sounded good—sure. But I didn't let my hopes take wing, because the reality was that there were several contenders for the license—the competition was keen. And it would probably take years for the FCC to make a decision and grant the license.

I agreed to help them with the initial license efforts, but I knew the rest was "iffy." After a few months, I completed the work for Steve and Darrell. They went back to their respective cities to finalize the license application and play the waiting game. We stayed in touch.

I wondered if anything would ever come from that endeavor. Casting those thoughts into the future where they belonged, I began to concentrate on the now—today.

"Where do I go from here, Lord?"

He opened a new door sooner than I expected.

I was offered a job as television specialist with the Texas Film Commission in the Office of the Governor. The six-person staff was doing an excellent job attracting filmmakers to Texas, but they needed someone to work directly with television production people.

I was brought on board to serve as the liaison between the commission and producers of television programs and commercials. Working for the Film Commission presented a new set of challenges. Now I was working behind the scenes in television, rather than on camera.

This was my first experience as a part of state government. Once I adjusted to dealing with the bureaucracy, it was smooth sailing. The hours were long and the demands great, but I liked the idea of embarking on a new adventure.

My favorite part of the job was traveling to New York, Chicago, and Los Angeles, calling on producers and selling them my terrific product—Texas!

Traveling within the state was gratifying, as well. The Visitors and Convention Bureau people throughout Texas were vital to our

Governor Bill Clements and wife Rita (second and third from left) with the Texas Film Commission staff.

success. They assisted us in finding ideal locations for productions and in luring producers to the state. Working with them was sheer delight and brought me many new friendships.

Some of the most fun included visiting the sets of movies and TV commercials being shot in Texas. My background in TV was definitely a plus in bringing credibility to my position. Directors and producers knew I was savvy about their problems.

Although there were only six of us with the Texas Film Commission—and we each had our areas of expertise—we all pitched in to help with the filming of *The Best Little Whorehouse in Texas*. All of us spent considerable time on the sets, especially when they filmed at the capitol. We enjoyed meeting Burt Reynolds, Dolly Parton, Dom Deluise, and all the other stars and were pleased with their cooperative spirit and friendliness to fans.

When the premiere of *The Best Little Whorehouse in Texas* rolled around, there was lots of hoopla. A TV crew was sent to do a special on the premiere and the parties. This was my department, and I was "Johnny-on-the-Spot" to assist them. One of the big parties was to be held at "the House" in Pflugerville, where the movie was shot. There would be a barbecue dinner, entertainment, dancing, and lots of stars and VIPs. And of course it would be videotaped to show on the coming TV special.

I was on my way home about 2:30 P.M. to get ready for the party, which started at 7:00 P.M., and decided to stop by the location to make sure everything was OK. Before I even got out of the car, the director rushed toward me with a desperate expression on his face.

"We have a tremendous problem. There's not ample electricity. You must get me a generator, and quickly!" he demanded.

I felt the blood drain from my face. Where in my job description did it say I was in charge of generators? Just what is a generator? And where do I get one? But I hid my inadequate feelings, put on my confident face, looked the director in the eye, and said, "I'll take care of it."

I raced to a phone and called the office, screaming, "Help!"

Executive assistant Joy Davis soothed my panicked state with serene reassurance that perhaps the National Guard could help. She told me to call the head honcho there, identify myself as being with the governor's office, then tell him about the emergency.

Premiere of The Best Little Whorehouse in Texas.

Jim Nabors, Dolly Parton, Governor Bill Clements, and Burt Reynolds welcome fans to The Best Little Whorehouse in Texas.

I did as she suggested, and within minutes I was assured a generator was on its way.

Hanging up the phone, I realized for the first time the clout afforded me by being in a division of the governor's office. I rushed back to the frantic director to inform him the generator was on its way. He smiled, hugged me, and said, "You're a genius—I love you—I love Texas!"

I drove home thinking, "This job's gonna work out just fine." Chily and I returned that evening for the festivities and had a fabulous time. Part of the fun came from viewing the vast amount of activity and knowing I had helped make it happen.

My duties at the Film Commission were varied and interesting and made me extremely resourceful. If we didn't have the answer or solution to a problem, we had to find it. It seemed to me that each new project presented challenges greater than the one before it.

Then there were the humorous moments. Remember the TV show *Real People?* The cast of that show provided me with one of the funniest and most outrageous experiences of my life.

As a promotion for the show, the producer decided the whole cast would take the Amtrak train from Los Angeles across the nation to Chicago, with whistle stops along the way to meet the American people.

Since the trip included stops throughout Texas, I helped with the arrangements. As a result, I was invited to join them on a portion of the journey. It was decided I would board the train in San Antonio and get off in my hometown—Taylor. I love trains, and getting to ride with Sarah Purcell and the others from the show made it that much more exciting.

We chugged along, stopping in New Braunfels, San Marcos, and Austin, but we were falling behind schedule. After leaving Austin, I asked the conductor what time we'd stop in Taylor.

His answer stunned me.

"Oh, we've decided not to stop in Taylor. We're just going to slow down and wave to the people, but not stop. If we stop there, we'll get farther behind schedule."

"But we have to stop there. That's where I live—I'm getting off there," I argued.

"Sorry, ma'am. The next stop is Temple."

"That's forty miles away. What am I supposed to do, walk home?"

"Nope. I guess we have only one option. When we slow down in Taylor, I'll get off. You'll be in the next car. When you get to me, you jump off, and I'll catch you. Then I'll get back on."

"You're kidding—right?"

"Nope."

"You want me to jump off this train while it's moving?"

"That's right. They do it all the time in the movies. Don't worry, I'll be there to catch you."

When we arrived in Taylor, amid shouts, cheers, laughter, and applause, I jumped—and thank goodness, he caught me!

Anything for the job.

CHAPTER 17

WALKING WITH THE LORD

Your religion is what you do when the sermon is over.
—"P.S. I LOVE YOU"

It was while I was at the Texas Film Commission that my spiritual life came into focus. With lots of time spent sitting in airports and flying, I had a chance to reflect on how God had brought me to this point.

When I heard stories about people who had moving religious experiences, I was in awe. I'd never had any great trauma that I could point to and say, "That moment changed my life."

My walk with the Lord has been a slow, tedious one. At times I tended to wander off, and He had to bring me back on track. I don't know how He could have been so patient with me.

But as I look back, I realize the Lord has guided me through every phase of my life. He has had a beautiful plan for my life—a mosaic where He and I still are filling in the pieces.

I know God has performed powerful acts to get my attention and has placed many special people in my life and spoken to me through them.

I joined the church when I was a teenager. No one talked me into it—it was my own decision. I joined because I believed in Jesus Christ, that He died for my sins, and that He rose from the dead.

I thought that because I believed those principles I was a Christian. But I really had no clue about the genuine commitment Christ was calling upon me to make. I thought, "Now that I'm a Christian, I'm on God's team. All I have to do is not kill, not steal or do any of those other 'thou shalt nots,' and God will reward me with a trouble-free, worry-free life." You know, the "live happily ever after syndrome." I was extremely immature, spiritually.

As a teenager, I lived a storybook life. I was very happy, a good student, included in everything, and I loved every minute of it. In college that scenario continued. I loved my major, enjoyed dating, and attending football games and other social events.

After graduating, enjoying my year's work in my field in the East and coming home and marrying my high school sweetheart, I thought I had the world by the tail.

Being a Christian is incredibly easy when everything's going your way, but the real test comes when things go wrong.

It wasn't until some years later that I gained insight and Christian understanding of death. I learned the lesson because God spoke to me through my five-year-old daughter.

Losing my beloved niece, Linda, still festered in my heart. Deep within my soul, I was still mad at God for allowing that beautiful, innocent child to die. Unknowingly, daughter Cindi led me to a whole new way of looking at death.

My grandmother, Big Mama, lived with my parents. She was in a wheelchair, and she and Cindi had an unusually special relationship. Cindi loved to go visit Big Mama. Big Mama would sit on her bed and let Cindi ride in the wheelchair, or she'd take Cindi onto her lap and they'd ride and they'd talk and have a glorious time. It was pure joy to see the love and companionship between one so young and one so old.

But Big Mama died, and we had to explain to Cindi what had happened. She wanted to go to the funeral home and see her, but everyone advised us against taking such a young child to see someone she dearly loved lying in a casket.

But something inside me said it was okay, and Chily and I decided we would take her. We took her in and held her up and let her look at Big Mama. She just smiled.

When we got outside, I said, "Well, Cindi?"

"Mommy, I'm so glad Big Mama's dead."

"Why?"

"Because, she isn't stooped over anymore. She isn't crippled anymore. She can walk again. Mommy, just think, right now, she's up in heaven, walking with Jesus."

At that moment I understood there are different kinds of healing. For the first time, I understood the glorification of death.

From then on I had what you might call the "take it or leave it" religion. If you're familiar with Carolyn Hoffman's book *Bloom Where You Are*, she calls it "bellhop religion." You know, you call on the Lord when you need Him and then, when you don't need Him, you ignore Him.

I would give God control of my life for a while, and then if He didn't run it to suit me, I'd yank it back. I suppose I was growing a little, but I was still very much a baby Christian.

About that time I started my television career and life took on new dimensions, new directions. I really began to feel the Lord was working in my life. He had put me in a unique position of helping people, and that was a good feeling. There are so many illustrations, some of which I have already mentioned, one in particular being the lady who saved the little girl from choking.

I discovered the Lord even works through commercials.

I made numerous public service commercials for non-profit organizations and I did one for United Way. It started out something like this.

"Hello, I'm Carolyn Jackson. I hope you're not having any difficulty in your life today, but if you are, there's help for you."

Then I went on to explain how people could get help. I gave the phone number and then said if there's a problem in your life or something's wrong, you should call this number.

One day, Beverly Scarbrough, the United Way's public relations person, called me.

"Are you sitting down?"

"Yes."

"Well, I have something to share with you and you need to be sitting down. We got a call from a lady who said she was about to commit suicide. Her husband had gone off and left her, and she had two small children and no job and no skills.

"Life seemed hopeless to her and she thought she'd be better off dead and letting someone else raise her children. But she loved them so much and wanted to watch them grow up. However, she was in that hopeless stage. The children had the TV on and your commercial came on. The lady thought to herself, 'There's help for me. I believe her, because she seems to be a friend.'

"So she called the hotline number, and we got help to her. The United Way is helping her get back into the mainstream of life again." I sat there and listened and shivered and cried and thanked the Lord.

But I don't think I gave Him all the glory. I think I kept some of it for myself. I'd ride high for a while, but then when things went wrong, I'd say, "Where are you, God? Why did you let this happen to me?"

There was a certain restlessness in my life, a lot of anxiety, even some hostility that I couldn't explain. I wanted everyone to change. Everyone except me. After all, there was nothing wrong with me. Outwardly, I had a great life. I had this tremendous TV job. There were a lot of people out there who admired me and looked up to me. I had a wonderful family who loved and supported me. Yet for some reason, I felt this nagging anxiety inside.

Then a friend invited us to a Bible study. When I asked Chily if he'd like to go, he wasn't too enthusiastic, but since nothing much was happening on Tuesdays, he said he guessed we could attend. We went and then returned a second and third time. I was absolutely amazed at how little I knew about the Bible. We had the Bible in our home all my life, yet I knew so little about the book.

You don't go out and play tennis without knowing the rules. But here I'd been playing the game of life without knowing the principles. I began to look around me and I saw some people who had something I didn't. And I wanted it. I hungered for knowledge of the Bible. I wanted to know about God's principles—how He speaks to me through His Word for my day-to-day living. I wanted to know what the Bible said about marriage.

One day our Bible teacher talked about ups and downs, about light and darkness, and I was so embarrassed, because I thought he was talking directly to me, describing my life. My life had been a roller coaster, up and down, up and down. Up on cloud nine one minute, down in the depths the next.

It dawned on me. You get down in the dumps when you're not right spiritually. So I studied hard, trying to get right spiritually. I realized I had been standing on rights, and I had to yield those rights. I had to remove some causes of conflicts in my life, and that wasn't fun. I am very stubborn, and it's hard to admit that I could ever have made some mistakes and needed to ask forgiveness.

Chily and I began growing together spiritually. It was like getting married all over again, but this time we did it right. We set aside some time for Bible reading and prayer. That was a giant step for us, because our prayers up to this time had been limited to blessings before meals.

We truly started seeking the Lord's will in our lives. I started learning some Bible verses. I began seeing some real changes in Chily, and gradually, I began to see a few changes in me.

I stopped overreacting to my family or to situations at work. I wasn't overly sensitive as I had been in the past. My feelings weren't hurt as readily. I accepted circumstances and did not suffer lows as often as before. I learned to rely on the Lord and to put things in proper perspective.

CHAPTER 18

STEP BY STEP

Prayer changes things.
—CHRISTIAN POSTER

I first noticed a decided change in my life when I was out at the YO Ranch near Kerrville. This ranch is huge and is home to all sorts of exotic animals such as giraffes and ostriches and you name it.

I was with the Texas Film Commission at the time, and they were filming a commercial there. Since I was the TV specialist, I went out to visit with the technicians shooting the commercial and to see that everything went well. I had a hotel room in Kerrville and rented a car to drive out there, a distance of about thirty miles.

I spent the entire day and had so much fun that I stayed much later than I should have. It was about 9:00 P.M. when I left and very, very dark. The road from the ranch to the highway was quite long. I had to drive through a locked gate to get out on the highway. When I left, they gave me the combination to open the lock.

I drove nervously along that dark, winding, lonely dirt road. No moon or stars were shining and it was the darkest, blackest night I'd ever seen. I felt like I was in the African jungle because I knew all kinds of wild animals were roaming around in the blackness.

I reached the gate and there was an artificial moonlight-type light over it, but it really was not well lit at all. I got out of the car

135

and struggled with the lock, but I could not see the numbers well enough to dial the combination.

Petrified, I ran back and jumped in the car. There I was, out there in the wilderness by myself in the dark in a strange car, surrounded by wild animals. I could hear all sorts of weird noises and felt so alone. I rummaged around in the glove compartment and found some matches. I grabbed them, ran back to the lock, and struck a match, but I still couldn't see well enough to work the combination.

I jumped back into the car and locked all the doors. Turning on the headlights, I got as close to the lock with the car as I could, but I still couldn't see the numbers clearly. I was just about to hit the panic button.

Tears began to stream down my face when all of a sudden, I thought, "Wait a minute. Where is your faith?" I began to recall some of the scriptures I had been learning about casting all your cares upon Him, because He cares about you. I recalled one line, "The Lord is my help, I will not be afraid."

I bowed my head and began to pray.

"Lord, I have never been as frightened in my entire life, but I know You are here with me and are going to see me through this. I can't see those numbers, but You can and I just ask you, dear Lord, please guide my fingers and help me open that lock."

I got out of the car. Fear totally had left me, and I had all the confidence in the world that I could open that lock. I spun the dial around, it click, click, clicked, and the lock opened!

I hopped back in the car and drove through the gate, got back out and locked it, and drove back to the highway. I can't describe the exhilaration that filled me.

I was so happy, I sang hymns all the way back into Kerrville.

One real test of my faith came while I was on a trip to New York. I was to leave for home about 2:00 P.M. The night before, I had heard there was a big snowstorm coming. That morning I called the airport and they said the storm wasn't due until about 4:00 P.M. and flights were on schedule.

I thought, "I'm not going to have any trouble getting out." I went to the airport, and after I checked in, it got later and later and everyone could hear the storm roaring in. The airline canceled our flight, saying the plane on which we were due to fly out could not land because of the storm. The next thing I knew, they had closed the airport.

I called home to tell Chily not to meet me, that I wasn't going to make it. He suggested I try to get to a hotel as quickly as I could, then let him know where I was.

They told us at the airport that all the hotels in the area were completely filled, so my only chance was to get back into Manhattan. I had two friends who were still in a Manhattan hotel, so I figured if I could get back to them, they'd take me in, and I'd be okay.

A young girl sitting beside me appeared to be frantic. She asked me some questions, and I suggested we hail a cab and try to get back into the city. She was very young, in her early twenties, and had never traveled much. She lived in Connecticut and was on her way to visit her fiancé in Arizona.

We went out to catch a cab, along with millions of other people, but by now the storm had hit full force, and I'm talking real snow. It was termed "the blizzard of the century." After standing out there some forty minutes in the freezing cold and snow, we finally snagged a cab. I suspect it was the last one out.

On the way in, I asked the girl if she'd like to go with me to the hotel, where she was welcome to stay with me and my friends until we could get out of there. She said she had some relatives in upper New York State, and if she could catch a train, she could stay with them.

I asked the cab driver if the trains were still running and he assured me they were. So I asked him to take us to Grand Central Station. We made it into town and even came within a block of the hotel I was trying to reach. I was tempted to go straight there, but I wanted to help this young lady.

I thought, "If she were my daughter, and she was in this sort of distress, I would appreciate it if someone with more travel experience would help her." We arrived at Grand Central Station, but she didn't know how to go about catching her train. So I told her I would go in and help her.

I let the cab go, which was my first mistake. I should have asked the cabby to wait, but I didn't have much cash in my purse. I had some credit cards, but cab drivers don't take credit cards. I didn't know how long I might be there, or what might lie ahead, so I decided I'd better hang on to what cash I had. I went in with her, and we found the right train. I helped her on and hugged her good-bye.

I went back outside, but no way was I ever going to find another cab. By this time, it was about 7:00 P.M., very dark, and the snow was swirling and piling up in the streets. There were very few cabs running. In fact, there was hardly any public transportation except the subway.

I thought, "What am I going to do?" Momentarily, the old me came back and I got a little bit angry with God. I thought, "The first thing I have to do is get to that hotel." Well, it was ten blocks away and here I was carrying luggage—luckily, not heavy luggage, because I'm a very light traveler.

Fortunately, I had on a heavy, warm coat, a scarf, a hat, and boots. I started out on my ten-block trek. I was far from being in the best part of town, and I was terrified.

When I started walking against that snow, it was like in *Dr. Zhivago*. You may remember in that movie the snow just kept falling and drifting so it was an effort to pick up one foot and put it before the other, the snow was so deep.

I made it about five blocks and realized I couldn't go any farther. Spotting a little coffee shop, I ducked inside. It was so small, it didn't even have booths or tables, just a bar where one could sit and sip a cup of coffee. I sat down and nervously eyed the only other people in there—two drunks.

They immediately tried to pick me up.

"Where you goin', Honey?" one said.

"What's a cute thing like you doing out on a night like this?" the other leered.

A friend had always told me, "When you're in New York, act like New Yorkers and everybody will ignore you." So I tried to put on my New York face and act like I was a New Yorker. I was careful to keep my mouth shut, so they wouldn't hear my Texas accent. Then I looked down at my luggage and thought, "Sure, New Yorkers run around carrying luggage in snowstorms all the time."

I decided the best thing to do was just to wait them out, so I immersed myself in my appointment book and sat there sipping my coffee for a long, long time until they finally left. I thought, "Now, that was dumb. They're probably outside waiting for me and will grab me the minute I step out the door."

While I sat shivering in that coffee shop, my budding anger with God grew. The old me reared her head and I began to question God.

"Why are you letting this happen to me? I tried to help some-one, and now look what's happened to me."

Sometimes God allows these things to happen to us so we learn a very valuable lesson. That lesson is to rely on Him.

Even old independent me, who thinks I can do everything, had to realize I was totally helpless. I said to myself, "You've been going around speaking to Christian women's clubs all over Texas about your faith. Do you really believe what you said, or were you just talking?"

I thought, "Yes, I do believe. I really do believe I can cast all my cares upon Him, that I can trust in the Lord with all my heart, and lean not upon my own understanding. The Lord is not limited by circumstances. With Him, nothing is impossible. Faith isn't the absence of fear, it's the presence of the Lord."

Right there in that little coffee shop in New York City, in the midst of the blizzard of the century, I was so grateful for a Bible verse Chily and I had memorized: "I can do all things through Christ who strengthens me."

I knew the minute I remembered that Bible verse that I could make it to the hotel because the Lord was going with me every step of the way. I picked up my luggage, stomped out of that coffee shop, and started walking the last five blocks to that hotel.

You can't imagine how cold it was. Once, even though I wore gloves, my hands got so cold I dropped some of my luggage and almost didn't realize it. By the time I reached the hotel, I was nearly frozen and couldn't even open the front door. The doorman had to come and let me in. I was absolutely exhausted.

Stumbling inside, I lifted my eyes heavenward and gasped, "Thank you, God."

I must have been staring up at that tall, handsome young doorman, who didn't hear me right, because, smiling, he said, "You're welcome."

My friends were not there at the moment, but the hotel had an available room, and I was able to check in and thaw out. I called Chily and told him I'd made it safely to the hotel. He told me, after hearing I was caught in the storm, that he had called members of our church, and they had started a prayer chain for my safety.

I was stuck there for three days, but God and I handled it just fine.

CHAPTER 19

THE ROAD AHEAD

*You'll learn more about a road by traveling it than by
consulting all the maps in the world.*
—"P. S. I LOVE YOU"

Before my frigid experience in New York, I had never realized how
much effect enduring mental stress has on physical condition. A
couple of weeks after returning from that trip, I went to my doctor
for a checkup and told him about my experience. He listened to me
very carefully, then said, "You know, you have absolutely defied all
the statistics. I can't believe it.

"Your body was not acclimated to that situation. You were
frightened, and completely drained of your physical strength. You
had been battling anxiety and trauma, and especially at your age, it
was a miracle you did not have a heart attack."

"Hey, watch it, there, Doc. What do you mean, 'at my age'?" I
teased.

Yes, it was a miracle. God is still in the miracle business. God
doesn't promise to explain to us why traumatic experiences happen
to us, but He does promise He will be there to see us through them.

And for me, He has been there. He's shown me I'm never alone
in a difficult situation. When He allows an extraordinary trial, He
provides extraordinary strength and comfort to survive it.

I discovered God gives us special skills and strength to help those we love the most.

When my Mom had a stroke, one of the first things the doctor told me was that she would never talk again.

"Oh, really? Want to bet?" I challenged him.

I unearthed all my old flash cards and teaching aids and began to work with her, starting with thirty minutes per day, then increasing to forty minutes, then to an hour, and I taught my Mom to talk again. I will never, ever forget the wonderful day she was able to look at me and say, "I love you."

I learned that God is there for you when life pierces your heart in the most painful manner.

Up to that point, I had thought losing a job was the worst thing in the world that could happen to me, but that paled in comparison to the pain that losing loved ones caused me.

I think back to that time when I engaged in Bible study and was trying to focus on God and get my life in proper perspective. God was building my faith and firmly planting in my mind scripture promises from which I could draw strength. I was about to face the most traumatic ten years of my life, enduring one tragedy, hurt, and crisis after another. But God had prepared me.

First, our daughter Carol and our son-in-law Brian lost one of their newborn twin sons. Next my dad died. Then my precious sister-in-law died a long, lingering death from cancer. Shortly thereafter, my beloved foster brother dropped dead of a heart attack.

My mother's health was rapidly deteriorating, and my brother developed cancer. I lost them both within a short time. Finally, my eight-year-old grandson suffered a stroke, after which he endured a long recovery.

I felt like Chicken Little. The sky was falling. Often I prayed, "God, I know You promise not to give us more than we can bear, but I'm on the brink—I'm about to crack. Please let me know You are still with me."

Immediately, I would receive a letter of encouragement from a friend, a phone call from one of my daughters, letting me know how much I was loved, or an unexpected hug from my husband. God has delightful ways of reassuring us that everything is going to be okay.

A dear friend commented, "I don't see how in the world you've handled all these terrible things that have happened to you. I don't know how you've survived."

"I couldn't have, by myself. The Lord carried me all the way."

While I was on television, I discovered that for some strange reason people think being on TV makes you different—makes you immune to the hurts of the world. Little did they know what I was experiencing off camera.

I can thank God now for the hurts, because how could I ever understand or help someone who was hurting if I hadn't hurt myself?

My three years at the Film Commission added sparkling new facets to my life. I was especially grateful for the deep friendships I developed with Joel Smith, the director, Joy Davis, his assistant, and many television and film people across the nation.

But all too often, I would encounter a fan who would say, "We miss you on the air. Please come back." I must admit I missed broadcasting, too. Once again, a new manager was on the scene at KLBJ, and he decided to return the station to the talk show format.

Paul Pryor, Cactus Pryor's son, was very active at the station at the time. He was doing a talk show on the air, and management decided to further expand the format. Paul called me one day and asked if I'd have lunch with him and the station manager.

I met them for lunch, and they asked me to consider coming back to KLBJ to do a talk show. It was a very difficult decision to make. My job at the Film Commission was challenging and exciting, and I was enjoying it.

"Let's face it," I told myself. "Broadcasting is in my blood and I miss it." But my salary would be cut in half, and I would be contract labor instead of a station employee.

They wanted me to do a two-hour solo show. They caught me at a very vulnerable moment, because at that time my sister-in-law was dying of cancer. I knew she only had about six to eight months to live, and I wanted some time to be with her.

The idea of a part-time job instead of a full-time job was very appealing. So once again I went back to KLBJ and revved up my talk show. The format was pretty much the same. The new manager told me he wanted me to keep the magazine format, the informative show, and that the afternoon show would be the controversial one where they really let people sound off and the host could get into it with them—the type they have these days.

That's the way we worked it out. Anytime someone asked to be a guest on my show who I believed was too controversial, I'd pass them on to the afternoon host.

And anytime someone called him who he thought would fit better into my magazine format, he passed that guest to me.

We got along great and it was a good association. After I was there for a year, KLBJ decided to sponsor a Caribbean cruise, which they asked me to host. This was arranged and I went on the cruise. Chily went with me, and we spent a delightful week in the Caribbean with about twenty-five or thirty listeners.

We played the gracious hosts for KLBJ and had a wonderful time. I called in every day, and if it was a time when the show was on the air, I got to talk to the audience for a few seconds and tell them what I was doing, which was fun for the listeners.

When we got back, everybody on the cruise couldn't wait for Monday morning, because they knew I'd talk about the trip and how much fun we'd had.

But when I arrived at the station that morning, everything seemed strange.

Carolyn fields calls from listeners at KLBJ.

Sometimes I had a way of knowing when I walked into a situation that something was different. And this day felt definitely different. I passed a guy who was a disk jockey with KLBJ-FM. He looked at me and said, "What a rotten place this is!"

I looked at him and thought, "Hmm, he got up on the wrong side of the bed."

When I walked in, the program director came into my office. He said, "I need to talk to you. You're not going on the air today."

"Why not?"

"Because you're not going to do this anymore."

"Excuse me? What are you talking about?"

"We don't want you anymore. You're fired. You're through. We want a bitch. We want a professional bitch."

I could not believe my ears. I said, "I'd like to hear this from the manager."

"I think that's a good idea."

The two of us went in and sat down in the manager's office. He was very uneasy.

I said, "I understand that you don't want me anymore."

He said, "That's right." He started to mumble and grumble about the ratings.

I said, the ratings are not even out. You don't have any idea how well this show is doing."

He said, "Well, anyway, we want this show to be controversial."

"The program director said you want a bitch. Is that correct?"

"Yeah," he muttered.

Looking him directly in the eye, I said, "Thank you for recognizing that being a bitch isn't my style." And I walked out.

So ended my association with KLBJ, for the last time.

When I left the station that day, I once more turned to the Lord in prayer.

"Dear God, I know I'm supposed to thank You for all things, but it's getting harder and harder to give thanks for losing jobs. You've sustained me this far. Now please help me to accept this with dignity and to look forward to tomorrow with confidence, to rely on Your guidance and to make right choices. Amen."

Everything seemed to be pointing me in the direction of a travel career. I began organizing tour groups and serving as a tour director.

Then came an unexpected turn of events. Steve Beard called to tell me they'd been granted the license and KBVO, now KEYE, was to become a reality.

By the time the station hit the airwaves, my involvement had somewhat diminished, but they did want me to produce and host the weekly public affairs show and possibly do some public relations for the station.

This minimal participation was fine with me, because travel had become my first priority. The TV show would be taped, which meant I could tape several shows in advance, enabling me to work around my travel schedule.

Things went extremely well for a couple of years. Again, I had the best of two worlds. I was traveling all over the world and meeting new people, yet I still had my finger in the broadcasting pie.

But when events seem too good to be true, they usually are. Nothing lasts forever.

Our program director, with whom I had a terrific rapport, resigned to go elsewhere. Something about his replacement gave me bad vibes. He was well qualified, fairly young, handsome, but my intuition told me he was shallow and insecure. After a few months I realized my evaluation was right on target.

One day he called me into his office and in a giddy, goofy sort of way told me about a newcomer. He related the way this "cute chick" had zoomed up to the station in her sports car, swished into his office, and convinced him she adored my show and wanted to be a contributing reporter for my program. He thought this was a wonderful idea.

It didn't take a rocket scientist to figure out he was smitten with her and she with him, even though they both were married. And he made it quite clear that adding her to my program was not a suggestion, but a mandate.

I took her under my wing and tried to help her as best I could. I wanted her to be good. If she weren't, it would reflect badly on my program and the station.

I later learned from staff members that while I was helping her, she was telling the powers that be how difficult I was to work with. Meanwhile, our cozy couple was getting cozier and cozier. We had our own private soap opera going!

Upon returning from a trip to Israel, I arrived at the station to find that my last show had not been aired. They scrapped it and let the new woman do one all by herself.

I walked into "Mr. Right's" office to ask what was going on. He informed me she was doing such an outstanding job that he had decided to let her host the show—alone! He didn't need me anymore.

Why was I not surprised? Mostly because by now I had learned through experience about the nasty side of the broadcasting business.

I wrote Steve and Darrell a letter expressing my total disillusionment and disappointment in them. Of course, they didn't fire me—but they didn't save me, either. Why should they—I'd served my purpose for them.

Strangely enough, this time it didn't hurt quite as much. And I gave thanks to God for making me stronger and wiser.

Footnote: Mr. and Miss Right divorced their spouses, married each other, lost their jobs, divorced—who knows where they are now! No doubt you're thinking that was the end of TV for me—wrong! A year or so later, KVUE decided to air an 11:00 A.M. to noon news program called News at 11. The focus would be predominantly news with special features. Dick Ellis, with whom I'd worked at KTBC, and Mary Vance would co-host. Dick and I decided I should be the travel editor and do a bi-weekly segment. Why not? It gave me exposure that helped boost my trips.

Once again, things went well for about a year. But management at KVUE decided an hour of news midday was too much and canceled the show. No reflection on me—just a change in programming. I left behind warm friendships and good feelings toward KVUE.

I also left behind broadcasting—forever—but only after establishing a record. As of today, I'm the only local TV personality who has worked with all the major network stations in the Austin market—PBS, CBS, NBC, ABC and Fox.

Not bad for a freckle-faced girl from Taylor.

Meanwhile, new dimensions are being added to my life through travel—dimensions I never thought possible. I've white water rafted in Colorado, ridden a camel in Israel, danced the hula in Hawaii, tiptoed across glaciers in Alaska, absorbed the magic of the Orient, explored the palaces and cathedrals in Europe, and cruised to the remote corners of the earth.

You were right, Papa Young, the world is mine, and God is my American Express—I never leave home without Him. My TV stories you've read, but my travel tales are waiting in the wings.

Stay tuned!

ABOUT THE AUTHORS

CAROLYN JACKSON grew up in Taylor, Texas, where at an early age she had a curiosity about the world and a yen for being in the spotlight. She graduated form The University of Texas with a degree in broadcasting and also attended The University of Southern California, Northwestern University, and Trinity University.

After a brief career in radio broadcasting and advertising, she put her ambitions on hold to marry her high school sweetheart and raise her two daughters. Eventually, however, she emerged as one of Central Texas' most popular TV and radio personalities. During her twenty-year broadcasting career, she received many honors, includ-

ing being named one of Austin's Outstanding Women, cited by Toastmistress International Austin Chapter for remarkable communicative skills, and named to Who's Who of American Women. After leaving broadcasting, Carolyn began a career in travel.

Currently, she escorts travel groups throughout the world as a tour director and is a cruise consultant. She is also a public speaker and appears in TV commercials and films. In 1989 she won the title of MS Senior Texas and was runner-up for MS Senior America. Carolyn and her husband, Chily, live in Georgetown, Texas, and are actively involved with the many activities of five grandchildren and two great-granddaughters.

BARBARA BARRIER has lived in Georgetown, Texas, for the last twenty-three years, and she writes for the *Williamson County Sun*, specializing in features. Her journalism degree is from Baylor University.

She and her husband of forty-five years, Jesse, have three children—Melanie, Holden, and Gaybeth—and nine grandchildren.

This is her first book.